Praise for *After the Cheering Stops*

"Grant Feasel was my friend and my center when I was a quarterback for the Seattle Seahawks, but I had no idea about the hidden and tragic story that unfolded after he retired. I read *After the Cheering Stops* in one night. It's eye-opening, painful, and redemptive. I pray Cyndy's book opens people's eyes and helps us all live in transparency by asking for help no matter the pain and problems we face."

—Jeff Kemp, former NFL quarterback
and author of *Facing the Blitz*

"Football, lacrosse, soccer, and hockey parents need to read *After the Cheering Stops*. Cyndy's story is one any parent should take close to heart. Brain trauma in our children is not only preventable, but it's a parent's job to give our children all of the information they need before they make their sport decisions. This great read will help."

—Becky Johnson, coauthor of *This Is
Your Brain on Joy* and *Nourished*

"*After the Cheering Stops* is a heart-wrenching and transparent story about CTE and concussions. Cyndy Feasel is destined to become the Erin Brockovich of CTE for sounding the alarm of what concussions can do to a family."

—Julie Carobini, novelist and
author of *Walking on Sea Glass*

"When Grant Feasel was my center while I was a quarterback for the Seattle Seahawks, we were close as can be. 'The Fighting Feasel' was the consummate pro—diligent, accountable, responsible, and selfless. His hands were often bloodied, so much so that there would be blood on the ball he hiked to me, prompting us to joke that we could be blood brothers. But, all those collisions took their toll. I'm proud of Cyndy for standing up and talking about the intimate details of her life after Grant's playing days were done."

—Dave Krieg, former Seattle Seahawks quarterback

After the
CHEERING
STOPS

After the CHEERING STOPS

AN NFL WIFE'S STORY
OF CONCUSSIONS, LOSS, AND THE
FAITH THAT SAW HER THROUGH

CYNDY FEASEL

WITH MIKE YORKEY

NELSON
BOOKS

An Imprint of Thomas Nelson

Published in Nashville, Tennessee, by Nelson Books, an imprint of Thomas Nelson. Nelson Books and Thomas Nelson are registered trademarks of HarperCollins Christian Publishing, Inc.

Published in association with the literary agency of WordServe Literary Group, Ltd., www.wordserveliterary.com.

Thomas Nelson titles may be purchased in bulk for educational, business, fund-raising, or sales promotional use. For information, please e-mail SpecialMarkets@ ThomasNelson.com.

Unless otherwise noted, Scripture quotations are taken from *The Message*. Copyright © by Eugene H. Peterson 1993, 1994, 1995, 1996, 2000, 2001, 2002. Used by permission of Tyndale House Publishers, Inc.

Scripture quotations marked NKJV are from the New King James Version®. © 1982 by Thomas Nelson. Used by permission. All rights reserved.

Scripture quotations marked NLT are from the *Holy Bible*, New Living Translation. © 1996, 2004, 2007, 2013 by Tyndale House Foundation. Used by permission of Tyndale House Publishers, Inc., Carol Stream, Illinois 60188. All rights reserved.

ISBN 978-0-7180-8833-0 (eBook)

Library of Congress Cataloging-in-Publication Data

Names: Feasel, Cyndy, author. | Yorkey, Mike, author.
Title: After the cheering stops : an NFL wife's story of devastation, loss, and the faith that saw her through / by Cyndy Feasel, with Mike Yorkey.
Description: Nashville : Thomas Nelson, [2016]
Identifiers: LCCN 2016020385 | ISBN 9780718088309 (hardback)
Subjects: LCSH: Feasel, Cyndy,—Mental health. | Feasel, Grant, 1952—Mental health. | Brain—Concussion—United States. | Football players—United States--Biography. | Sports injuries—Patients—Biography.
Classification: LCC RC394.C7 F43 2016 | DDC 617.4/81044092 [B]—dc23 LC record available at https://lccn.loc.gov/2016020385

Printed in the United States of America

16 17 18 19 20   RRD   10 9 8 7 6 5 4 3 2 1

To Sean, Sarah, and Spencer, the true survivors of this story

CONTENTS

CONTENTS

A NOTE TO THE READER
FROM CYNDY FEASEL

I f I'd only known that what I loved the most would end up killing me and taking away everything I loved, I would have never done it."

These were among the last words spoken to me by my late husband, Grant Feasel. He was talking about playing professional football.

Grant was the starting center and long snapper for the Seahawks from 1987 to 1992 after starting his pro football career with the old Baltimore Colts in 1983. While playing 117 games in the National Football League, Grant was just another anonymous offensive lineman who toiled in the trenches, banging up his battered body with every snap of the ball. As you're about to read, those jarring collisions with powerful nose guards took their toll on Grant in physical, mental, and spiritual ways.

You see, Grant drank himself to death—a slow, lingering process that took nearly twenty years. He didn't press a gun to his heart and pull the trigger like San Diego Chargers linebacker Junior Seau did, but Grant committed suicide all the same. He drank to dull the pain that began in his brain—a brain muddled by a history of repetitive trauma and symptomatic concussions. He drank and drank . . . until the alcohol killed him.

Grant's death certificate lists "ESLD" (end-stage liver disease, a form of cirrhosis of the liver) as the cause of his demise, but our family later learned that he also suffered from a degenerative brain disease known as chronic traumatic encephalopathy, or CTE, which has been the focus of lawsuits from former NFL players and the topic of a Hollywood movie, *Concussion*, starring Will Smith.

And then there was the collateral damage. I can assure you that what happened to Grant during our adult years together destroyed our marriage, devastated my relationship with our three children, and left me destitute. All because he played a violent game that entertains tens of millions of football fans every Sunday.

What you're about to read will be difficult and raw in many ways, but I want to put a human face on what can happen to an NFL player and his family long after the cheering has stopped. My life and our children's lives became a living hell because of the way alcohol became his medication for a disease that had its roots in the scores of concussions he suffered on the football field. His helmet-to-helmet collisions opened the door to brain trauma that impacted his thought processes, accelerated his physical deterioration, and altered his personality. In the end, we realized that football had cost him everything—his life, his relationship with me, and his family.

Those are important points because the Grant Feasel I fell in love with and brought three children into this world with was not the Grant Feasel I said good-bye to at the age of fifty-two. My husband was someone I adored and respected, a godly man of character who wanted to be the best at what he did—until hits to the head and jarring of his brain resulted in a slow, steady progression of subtle changes to his personality, his work ethic, and his ability to think clearly.

Besides telling Grant's story, I also want to raise awareness for parents about the dangers of playing sports that produce concussions. I'm an art teacher at Fort Worth Christian School, a private Christian pre-K through twelfth grade school in North Richland Hills, Texas. As I write this book, a handful of my middle school students have missed up to a week of classroom instruction because of concussions they received while playing organized football and soccer. While many think that concussions are synonymous with football, the head-butting sport of soccer produces the most concussive events by virtue of its popularity and the fact that both boys and girls play the sport.

In addition, a study published in the *American Journal of Sports Medicine* showed that girls playing soccer experienced concussions at nearly *twice* the rate of boys. And if you played contact sports in high school and were concussed, then you need to be aware that you could be traveling down the same road that Grant trod—especially if you are using alcohol or prescription drugs to dull those lingering aches and pains.

Finally, I want to make this point: I know that Grant would not want his name to be remembered this way, but I also know that he would want me to warn others about the dangers of CTE. He always admired the way I could talk to anyone about anything, and he liked me to fill in the gaps for him with groups of people.

I consider *After the Cheering Stops* to be a continuation of a relationship that started with such promise but ended so tragically.

CHAPTER 1

NO DEFENSE AGAINST STRESS

It was my therapist who suggested that I start journaling.

I was going through a rocky, unsettled time in my life when my husband, Grant, was constantly drinking and barely hanging on to his job. His addiction to alcohol brought unbelievable stresses on our marriage and produced deep anxiety among our three children who ranged in age from their early twenties to high school.

My therapist said that keeping a diary-like journal would be an effective stress-management tool and would present me with the opportunity to explore my feelings while gathering thoughts about my life, which was a mess. With that idea in mind, I began journaling in 2007 as a way to process the traumatic developments in my life and release any pent-up emotions and frustrations.

It wasn't easy dealing with an alcoholic husband while trying to maintain a steady home environment for our three children, Sean, Sarah, and Spencer. There were other stresses as well: shielding Grant's addiction from our extended family, managing the demands of a full-time teaching position, and keeping the bills paid. We lived in a five-bedroom, five-bath traditional brick home in Colleyville, an affluent suburb near the Dallas/Fort Worth International Airport. Even though residing in Colleyville—or "Colleywood," as my kids joked—was like living in a bubble, there was a darkness inside our home at 7003 Orchard Hill Court. Consider this journal entry from April 2010:

> My life is over as I know it. The past 17 years with Grant have gone downhill. For the past 30 days, he's been drinking heavily. Now he's drinking in the middle of the day. Grant promised that if he relapsed he would go to a treatment center. We are all very afraid.

My entry continued with a description of what happened between Grant and me that Monday morning. I awoke at my usual 6:00 a.m., knowing that I needed to drive Grant to a nine o'clock appointment with a psychiatrist, Dr. Ernest Brown (not his real name). I had already informed the school administration that I would be taking a personal day. I couldn't trust Grant to drive himself to the doctor's office.

Grant used to be an early riser—dating back to his early morning workouts for football—but that all changed when he started drinking morning, noon, and night in the last couple of years. There were times when he struggled to get out of bed at all.

That morning, I wondered if he'd had so much alcohol the previous day and night that he'd have trouble waking up in time for his appointment. Because of his deteriorating condition, I was anxious for him to see the doctor. For weeks I had pleaded, "Grant, you have to see Dr. Brown! You're depressed. You need to see a psychiatrist."

Grant's father had died a couple of months earlier, sending my husband into a deep emotional tailspin. I know Grant felt guilty because he had interacted with his family less as alcohol took control of his life. I closed my eyes and recalled the touching and emotional memorial service for DeWayne Feasel. It was a beautiful day in Grant's hometown, the high desert city of Barstow, California, a hundred miles east of Los Angeles in the middle of the arid Mojave Desert.

Inside the chapel at Mead Mortuary, the words of old hymns like

"I Come to the Garden Alone" and "The Old Rugged Cross" caused me to cry as I squeezed Grant's hand. Then my oldest son, Sean, read the Twenty-Third Psalm with its haunting line: "Yea, though I walk through the valley of the shadow of death, I will fear no evil" (NKJV). Throughout the service, Grant was frail and shaky; his skinny hand felt small as I grasped it tightly and sobbed.

Grant, Sean, and Spencer were pallbearers and wore white gloves. I silently prayed Grant would hold up. During the internment ceremony at Mt. View Memorial Park, with the beautiful desert mountains like a perfectly painted backdrop, I stood and sobbed uncontrollably. I wasn't crying for my seventy-eight-year-old father-in-law, who'd been given a long life. Instead, I couldn't help but think that Grant would be next.

In the days and weeks following the memorial service, the amount of alcohol Grant drank on a daily basis escalated. Even though Grant had always been a "closet drinker"—someone who did his best to hide his drinking—he was only fooling himself. As much as he tried to conceal his affair with alcohol from me and the kids, the physical toll couldn't be missed: Grant's footing wasn't sure, he stammered and stuttered, his hands trembled, and his eyes remained glassy 24-7. This was the "new normal"—the natural evolution of a forty-nine-year-old alcoholic who began drinking regularly when his pro football career was over.

Grant started out as a Crown and Coke guy—pouring Crown Royal Canadian Whisky into a Big Gulp–sized cup mostly filled with Diet Coke. Then he switched to mixing Jack Daniel's, the popular Tennessee whiskey, with whatever was on hand—orange juice, cranberry juice, or Diet Coke. After 2005, he became an Absolut Vodka drinker, adding the potent Swedish vodka to Diet Sprite. He had to give up drinking caffeinated Diet Coke after an anxiety issue landed him in the emergency room. Because his stomach bothered him—a symptom of poor nutrition and a liquid-only diet—he started mixing the vodka with Gatorade, a sports drink favored by athletes.

It was becoming clear that the alcohol was taking a huge toll on Grant, and he needed help. I don't know how I talked him into agreeing to see a psychiatrist since we disagreed on just about everything, but he said yes. On this particular morning, however, he barely moved in bed, so I gave him a good shake, which he didn't appreciate.

"Okay, okay," he said, shielding his eyes from the bright sunlight filling our bedroom. We were having another beautiful spring morning.

I watched him struggle to get upright. At six feet seven inches tall, Grant was a giant compared to most men, but he was far from his playing weight of 295 pounds. He looked to be a rail-thin 240 pounds, a result of the empty calories he received from consuming alcohol-spiked drinks throughout the day.

Grant drank constantly from a forty-four-ounce Styrofoam cup with a red-and-yellow logo from Sonic Drive-In. He would withdraw to his home office and fill and refill his mega-sized "Route 44" cup with Diet Sprite and Absolut Vodka throughout the day. Just the sound of a pop-top being pulled would tell me that the alcohol was flowing. Come bedtime, he'd set his Route 44 on the nightstand, topped off and readily available to drink from during the night. It was all about maintaining the buzz—and never having a hangover.

"We only have an hour before we have to—"

"Leave me alone," he said. Grant didn't like me hovering around his space. He constantly ridiculed me for "micromanaging" him, and he resented how I hunted down bottles of Absolut Vodka that he hid in his office drawers or stashed in his huge walk-in closet's minifridge—which had a combination lock that he had added.

Whenever I found his booze, I poured the big bottle of vodka—1.75 liters—down the bathroom sink. When he caught me doing that, he usually went ballistic, yelling at me about wasting another forty bucks we didn't have.

On this particular morning, I looked at my husband's gaunt face and glazed eyes. "Grant, please get ready," I said. With that, I left to get myself my morning coffee.

A half hour later, Grant staggered into the kitchen, dressed in his usual around-the-house attire—a loose-fitting, long-sleeved Nike T-shirt and Nike navy-blue sweatpants. He was so skinny that he looked swallowed up in his clothes.

Now that he was on his feet, I got a better measure of how he was doing. Grant was drunk—at eight thirty in the morning. He must have been sipping Diet Sprite and vodka throughout the night or taken long gulps after I left our bedroom.

"Where are my keys?" he demanded.

"I've got them." I held up the keys, which I had started hiding whenever I thought he was too drunk to drive. I couldn't live with myself if he got behind the wheel. "You're not driving anywhere in your condition. I told you last night that I'll drive." I was adamant.

Grant wasn't having it. "I'm driving myself!"

"No, you're not. I'm driving."

I wasn't going to argue with someone who was in no shape to get behind the wheel. I stepped through the garage and onto our driveway, where Grant's company car—a run-of-the-mill Ford Taurus—was parked.

Grant chased after me. "Give me those keys!"

I was gripping the car keys in my right hand when Grant wrestled me for them. We pushed and pulled, neither of us giving in until Grant wrenched them out of my hand, the metal key ring scraping my fingers and causing them to bleed. The keys fell to the pavement, and I let out some sort of scream from the pain. My heart was beating fast; I was afraid.

I didn't care if the whole neighborhood saw us. This wouldn't have been our first public quarrel anyway. Grant scooped up the keys, opened the car door, and sat down in the driver's seat. Then he sat there, too drunk to process what to do next. We had an automatic gate to our driveway, and there were times when he couldn't remember how to open the gate.

I ran back inside the house and called for our oldest child.

"Sean, you have to come help me with Dad! He's trying to drive himself to the doctor, and he's drunk."

Sean came running from his upstairs bedroom. Twenty-five years old at the time, our son had graduated from Abilene Christian University and lived in Austin. He came home for a long weekend because he knew I'd been having a lot of problems with Grant and needed backup. When the two of us reached the driveway, I was relieved to see that Grant had stepped out of the car, although I had no idea why.

Sean, who was strong-willed, took charge. "Dad, you're not driving. You're in no shape to do this."

Grant didn't see what the problem was. "There's nothing wrong with me. I can drive."

"No, Dad. Give me the keys—now."

My son spoke with a firm-but-under-control voice. Then Sean reached for the keys, and father and son tussled for a moment. Sean wasn't as tall as Grant, but he was a stout six feet and had played defensive back at ACU, the same school where Grant had played his college ball.

Their grappling was short-lived. Sean seized the car keys from Grant's clasp and told his father, "Get in the car. I'm driving."

I breathed a sigh of relief as the Ford Taurus pulled out of the driveway. As I watched our son and my drunken husband leave the neighborhood, I thought about how we had gotten to this tragic point in our lives and our marriage.

Since he retired from the NFL, Grant had a sales position with Fujifilm Medical Systems, a manufacturer of digital X-ray and mammography equipment. He mainly worked out of his home office, although he'd also go on the road to meet and take care of his clients. Most of the time, though, he holed up in his office off the master bedroom, answering e-mails and returning sales calls. The lack of managerial supervision meant that Grant could get an early start on his Route 44s.

Right around the time that Grant's father died on January 30, 2010, my husband told me that I couldn't call him on his work phone because someone in human resources was after him.

"After you for what?" I asked.

"I don't know. They're trying to get me and give someone else my job! I know they're looking at my phone and the text messages you send me. Don't talk about my drinking in your text messages!"

Grant was clearly paranoid that someone in HR would find out about his addiction to alcohol. And the filter that protected him from using bad language in public and with our kids was impaired as well.

One night I was at the gym working out when our daughter, Sarah, went into the master bathroom to borrow my fingernail polish. Grant heard her making some noise and confronted her.

"What the @#$% are you doing here?" he roared. "Get the @#$% out of my bathroom!"

Sarah had never been spoken to in such a manner. When she heard her father drop the f-bomb on her, she was momentarily stunned and then started crying hysterically. She ran out of the bathroom in tears and called me at the gym to tell me the story. She was still upset when I arrived home.

When I went to talk to Grant about how he treated Sarah, he was drunk and half-asleep in our bed. He said he thought HR was breaking into the house. This type of odd behavior had been building for a long time. Paranoia about people out to get him, using vile language, and hands that shook like he had full-blown Parkinson's—Grant needed serious help.

Since my efforts to convince him to enter rehab had fallen on deaf ears, I tried a different tactic: perhaps he would agree to see a psychiatrist. Maybe a shrink could unearth any genetic, physiological, psychological, or social factors behind his problem drinking. When he said yes to my suggestion, I thought we were moving in the right direction.

After the driveway scuffle, Sean drove him to his appointment with Dr. Brown. I wasn't there, but I do know this: instead of noticing that my husband was drunk in the middle of the morning—and sending him straight to a rehab facility like I hoped—the psychiatrist asked a few basic questions and handed my husband a prescription for Prozac, an anti-depressant, and Xanax, an antianxiety medication. In other words, all the "help" my husband received were two bottles of mood-relaxing pills, which are easy to become addicted to and easier to abuse—especially if you take them in conjunction with alcohol.

A week later, I saw the bottle of Xanax near his bathroom sink. I shook it—empty. One hundred potent antianxiety pills were gone in less than seven days.

I called Dr. Brown's office and spoke with a nurse. "I'm Grant Feasel's wife, and I'm sure he said that I can't talk to you, but I want Dr. Brown to know that Grant's going to end up dead from those prescriptions he gave him. My husband is mixing them with vodka."

The nurse stopped me. "He's drinking with those?"

"Yes. He's taking those pills with vodka. The entire prescription for Xanax you gave him a week ago is gone."

"Okay, Mrs. Feasel. I'll put a red flag on his folder and make sure when he comes in next time that Dr. Brown discusses this with him."

The next time Grant saw Dr. Brown, my impaired husband left the office with a different antianxiety prescription in hand—for Klonopin, which turned out to be something new to mix with Grant's vodka-spiked Gatorade. When I called Dr. Brown's office, I was put through to the psychiatrist, who said that he had told Grant that he needed to get into a rehab facility *quickly*. Grant never told me about that conversation.

And then Grant was hit by another thunderbolt—the sudden death of his good friend Keli McGregor, who was just two years younger than he. Keli and Grant were teammates on the Seattle Seahawks and got on so well that Keli's wife, Lori, and I called them soul mates. Keli was a wonderful Christian man of high character and a magnetic personality who drew people to him.

Our bond continued after football was over. We saw Keli and Lori occasionally in Texas and cheered Keli's move into baseball when he became the senior director of operations for the Colorado Rockies in 1993. Keli proved to be an excellent administrator and was ultimately named president and CEO of the Rockies in 2001. We couldn't have been happier for him and his family.

Here's where Keli's story takes an interesting twist: Back in 1996, Keli was instrumental in the hiring of Grant's brother, Greg, as the Rockies' vice president of sales and marketing, and Greg has worked in the front office ever since. Then on April 20, 2010, Keli was in a Salt Lake City hotel room on a routine business trip for the Rockies when he suddenly died of a heart attack. He was forty-seven years old.

The news of Keli's death descended like a thick fog upon my husband, who was weakening each day from depression.

I wrote this in my journal:

> Grant's lost.
> I miss him.
> I'm lonely.

In the midst of my pain, I recalled the last time that I saw Keli. It had been a couple of months earlier when he flew to California for DeWayne's funeral. He honored the family by offering a heartfelt prayer during the memorial service.

After the internment, Keli found me in the crowd and pulled me aside. I immediately noticed the great worry in his face.

"Cyndy, something's wrong with Grant," he said. "What is it? What's going on with him? His hands are shaking, and I've watched how he keeps them in his pockets so others don't notice, but I have.

I'm worried about him! He doesn't look well. He's too thin. Just tell me what's wrong."

I wish Keli and I could have had a few minutes of privacy so that I could tell him everything. "I can't talk here," I said. "Let me call you in a few days."

"That's a promise," Keli said, a look of concern still etched in his expression.

"Yes, that's a promise."

Due to Grant's deterioration, I never made that phone call, and we never spoke again. Then came the shocking news of Keli's sudden and unexpected death.

His words haunt me to this day.

LOSING CONTROL

A few weeks later, on Sunday, May 2, 2010, Grant went to church with me for the first time in months.

I was raised in the church—and so was Grant. We had that common bond, so I was encouraged when he joined me to worship at Gateway Church, a nondenominational congregation. Perhaps we were turning a corner.

I could tell that Grant had been drinking that morning, but I kept my thoughts to myself to maintain peace between us. We took separate cars because Sarah—who was attending the University of North Texas but living at home—and I were planning to go out to lunch and see a movie together after church. We both said we needed some "girl time."

Inside Gateway, the three of us sat together, and I noticed that Grant raised his hands and arms while the worship band played with great emotion. That was totally out of character for him, and he also sang loud—way too loud. I didn't know what to think.

When the service was over, Sarah whispered in my ear, "Dad's drunk. He's acting weird."

We couldn't make a scene at church, so all we could do was watch Grant drive away. We were both very upset about him driving drunk. He did it regularly though.

Sarah and I got in my car, and we had a good cry. Then I called my sister and father and told them how afraid I was about the situation. What was happening was insane—and I felt powerless to do anything about it. Life was spinning out of control for him and for the rest of us.

That evening, I wrote this entry in my journal:

When Sarah and I came home from the movie, Grant must have mixed meds with his vodka because he was totally out of it. That night, he fell once again into the nightstand, crushing the lampshade and knocking all the pictures off the wall, along with a huge Gatorade bottle full of vodka. He also wet our bed.

Nighttime was worse with Grant for several reasons. By then, the accumulation of vodka in his system was at its highest—and his ability to be cognizant or maintain physical control of his body was at its lowest. More than once I heard him stir in the night and waked to the sight of him standing at the foot of our bed—and peeing onto our bedding and mattress.

The first time I witnessed this bizarre behavior in the middle of the night, I asked him, "What are you doing?"

"I'm going to the bathroom."

"Grant, you're peeing on our bed."

"Oh."

That's how out of it Grant was. Each time he soaked our sheets, I flipped on a light switch and got out another set of sheets for our king-size bed.

My next journal entry was from May 5, 2010, written when our youngest child, Spencer, was finishing his sophomore year at Fort Worth Christian.

Spencer and I were coming up to the house when we saw two police cars in front of our home. As we drove up, two policemen were loitering at our front door.

"What's going on?" I asked.

One of the cops replied, "We're looking for Grant Feasel."

"I'm his wife."

"Ma'am, we got a call from a coworker of Grant's who said she was afraid for his safety. She said he sounded very depressed on the phone, and there were loud noises in the background. Do you have any guns in the home, ma'am?"

"No, I don't believe so."

"Can you let us in?"

"Of course."

I'll admit to feeling icy fear when we stepped into the quiet house. We found Grant in the master bedroom, lying perfectly still on our bed and totally out of reality. That night, I wrote this in my journal:

After the cops leave, Grant falls two or three times really badly. He tried to have a phone call but dropped the phone, which sounded like a gunshot when it hit the hardwood floor. I am terrified that he is going to hurt himself seriously. He just crashed into the bathroom door and knocked a hole in the wall. Earlier, it was a broken office door handle and a broken fax machine.

I have a picture on my phone of Grant drunk, passed out on the carpet. He fell out of bed and hit his head and ribs. He told me the next morning that I'd broken his ribs. God help us.

How low could he go? How horrible could things get?

This was not the life or the marriage I expected when I met a tall, blond, and good-looking football player from California on the Abilene Christian University campus.

The football player who wanted to become a dentist.

CHAPTER 2

OPENING DRIVE

I didn't go to many football games my first two years of college, even though I attended a four-year university in the great state of Texas, where football is king.

But I sure went to a lot of games after I met a golden boy from California who was playing on the Abilene Christian University football team.

It was my roommate Janna Masch who introduced me to Grant Feasel during the summer of 1981 before the start of my senior year. I was attending summer school at Abilene Christian and had recently broken off a relationship with a guy who I had been dating exclusively for a year, and Janna thought I could benefit from jumping right back into the dating pool. She wanted to cheer me up because I wasn't my usual perky self after the emotionally difficult breakup.

"You need to get over this guy," she said. "You've got to move on, date someone else. Tell you what. I have a friend, and I want you to meet him." Janna also knew that Grant had been in a serious relationship and was on the rebound, too, so she was trying to help out both of us.

I rolled my eyes. "Who is he?"

"Do you know the Feasel brothers?"

On a campus of four thousand undergraduates, it was impossible to know everyone, but I had heard of Greg and Grant Feasel from California.

15

They were brothers on the Abilene Christian football team my sophomore year, and they were both tall and huge. I remembered them looking like twin towers—a pair of Greek gods with helmets of wavy hair when they walked across the campus quad. They were standout athletes who had made names for themselves. But I wasn't one of those girls who really knew a lot about football players at ACU.

I told Janna that I had met Greg, the older Feasel, but I couldn't remember under what circumstances.

"Well, I'm talking about Grant, and he's a nice guy like his brother," Janna replied. "Let me ask him to come over to the house some afternoon. You two can visit, and if you don't like him, then you don't have to go out with him."

"Okay," I said. "I'm up for anything."

I was a free spirit and liked new experiences, but if I was being honest with myself, I didn't like being down in the dumps after breaking up with the other guy. Maybe this Grant Feasel would be an interesting person to meet. What did I have to lose?

A few days later, on a blazing hot afternoon in July, Grant dropped by the house I was sharing with four girls. He drove up in an old, beat-up white truck. When he stepped out of the cab and I got a good look at him, I thought he was fantastic looking. He was big, blond, and tan from working outside all summer. His dark skin, light hair, and rugged good looks said "California sunny boy" to me.

He didn't fit the mold of most guys at Abilene Christian, who had the cowboy look going: West Texas jeans, cowboy boots, Stetson hats, and western yoke shirts with piping. Grant? He wore Levi's 501 button-up jeans that hung on his long, lanky hips just so, a loose-fitting button-down shirt, and flip-flops. I didn't know anyone who wore flip-flops at ACU, but Grant did. He also looked as strong as an ox; he was muscular and had no fat on his lean Olympian physique.

I invited Grant inside to meet my roommates, and he charmed

everyone with his gentle smile and easygoing ways. One of my room-mates had a record player, and she was playing her favorite albums, so we started talking about what types of music we liked.

Grant really lit up. "I love Jackson Browne," he said. "'Running on Empty,' 'The Pretender,' 'Rock Me on the Water,' and 'The Load Out'—those are great songs."

I was happy to hear that Grant was a big fan of classic rock and told him that was my favorite music too. When he declared his appreciation for country music, I said I felt the same way and that I loved great country artists like Johnny Cash and George Jones.

Music was a great connector for us. I was further intrigued when he told me that he liked to play the guitar and piano. This guy wasn't a dumb football player. He was much more well-rounded than the stereo-typical jock.

"That's awesome," I said. "I played the piano growing up, but I wasn't great at it."

We must have chatted for a good hour or so on the couch while my roommate changed albums on the record player. I liked what he had to say. He was soft-spoken, kind, calm, and cute. His relaxed manner was completely different from mine. I had a lot of energy, and my friends would say I was loud.

When he had to go, I thanked him for dropping by. Grant asked me for my phone number, and in those pre–cell phone days, I gave him the number to the house.

An hour or so later, our phone rang. It was Grant, sounding a bit shy.

"Hey, I had a nice time meeting you today," he began. "Would you like to go out to dinner? I know this hamburger place."

"Sure!" I replied. "When?"

"How about tonight?"

This guy was moving quickly. But what girl would say no to that invitation?

"I need some time to get ready . . ." I wanted to make sure I looked good. My heart was beating fast, an indication that I was excited.

"Would an hour be enough?"

"That would be wonderful. See you then."

When he arrived, Grant opened the car door for me, and the first thing he did was pop in a cassette tape of Neil Young's *Heart of Gold*, an album that was nearly ten years old. Neil Young's acoustic guitar and harmonica became the soundtrack to the start of our romance.

Over cheeseburgers and fries, we carried on a good conversation. Well, maybe I did most of the talking since I'm the bubbly sort. I can talk a lot, and sometimes I overpower people. I can be very direct, and most of the time I say exactly how I feel.

Grant didn't seem to mind listening to me, and when he did speak up, he had something to say. He made it known to me that he was a Christian. Hearing him say that really impressed me, because if our relationship was going to go any further, that commonality was a prerequisite.

As the evening moved along, we shared stories of how we grew up.

A *LEAVE IT TO BEAVER* CHILDHOOD

I was raised in Garland, Texas, the oldest of David and Martha Davy's three daughters. Garland, part of the Dallas-Fort Worth Metroplex, was a comfortable, middle-class community of eighty thousand residents with wide streets, greenbelts, and large brick homes. Dad was a graphic designer and artist who founded his own company that was very successful. He did brochure work for Texas Instruments, an electronics company that was the Apple and Microsoft of its day.

Mom was content to be a stay-at-home mom and call herself a homemaker. She used to put on a nice dress and freshen up her makeup when Dad was coming home from work, and it was important to her to have a hot meal waiting on the table. She respected Dad and loved him, and they weren't bashful about holding hands or kissing each other in front of us kids. They were high school sweethearts still deeply in love with each other.

I was born on September 20, 1959, and had a perfect childhood—no crashing waves or rocky turbulence. When I heard about divorce and family problems from other kids, I thought, *Whoa, I have a sheltered life.* I lived a happy childhood in a safe, secure environment, often playing with the neighbors until the sun went down.

Every Sunday morning and evening—*and* Wednesday nights—my parents took us to the Saturn Road Church of Christ, where Dad was an elder. One of the things he insisted upon was that there would be no alcohol in the house. His mother was an alcoholic, so Dad had seen what alcohol could do to a home. He wanted to be sure we were raised in a calm, peaceful environment.

After I attended neighborhood elementary and junior high schools, my parents thought I should be influenced by teachers and students who held a similar worldview as theirs, so they enrolled me and my younger sisters, Lori and Alisa, into Dallas Christian School in Mesquite, a half hour south of Garland. Dallas Christian School was affiliated with the Church of Christ.

I was a bundle of energy at Dallas Christian. Being a cheerleader and singing in the school choir helped burn off some of that feistiness. My parents never knew what to do with me because I was rambunctious and liked to be involved in everything. In Texas terms, I was a budding socialite.

I had lots of friends and was voted homecoming queen my senior year. My closest friends were two boys—Bobby Babbitt and Mike Hoover. We had fun hanging out together—mostly at my house—and going to Texas Ranger baseball games. Even though we spent a lot of time in each other's company, I didn't date either of them. I did go out with other guys after I was allowed to date at age sixteen.

I was a good kid, and things like drinking and drugs weren't part of my vocabulary. I never hung out with classmates who drank or smoked pot. Instead, my friends and I would go to the movies or sit around a restaurant table talking and having fun.

During my senior year, I had to start thinking about college. My parents definitely wanted me to continue my education and get a degree—especially Mom, who didn't go to college. I was really good at art, having inherited that gene from my father, so I thought about doing something with that. Plus, I loved kids. I'd taught at Sunday school, Vacation Bible School, and church camp, so I thought there might be a way to connect art and kids in some fashion.

But I wasn't sure what to study in college or what major to pursue. I halfheartedly applied to North Texas State, East Texas State, and Abilene Christian University. They were all fairly close to home, but I didn't have the desire to go far from home anyway. I really thought I'd end up going to nearby Eastfield Junior College since I wasn't sure what to study.

At the end of my senior year, when it was time to decide, my best girlfriend Suzy Rudd said she had committed to Abilene Christian. She knew I had applied and been accepted. "I don't have a roommate," she said. "Why don't you go to ACU with me and we'll room together in the dorms?"

That was all the push I needed. "Great!" I immediately replied.

And that's how I decided to attend Abilene Christian University. The tuition costs were higher at ACU than at a state school, but my parents were fine with that. We had visited the campus and knew many other people who'd gone to Abilene Christian, so our comfort level was high. Plus, ACU was founded by members of the Church of Christ back in 1906 and maintained a close affiliation with our denomination. Students were required to attend daily chapel and take several Bible courses before graduation. Freshmen and sophomores were also required to live in student dorms.

Rooming with Suzy was great. I loved being in college, and I made good grades as an education major with a minor in art. After two years in the dorms, I was glad to move into a rental house with three girls, including my matchmaker Janna Masch.

GROWING UP IN THE DESERT

Grant told me about his hometown during our first date.

"I grew up in Barstow," he said.

"Barstow? Where's that?"

"In California."

I immediately pictured swaying palm trees with the azure blue Pacific Ocean as a backdrop. My parents had taken us to Disneyland and the Los Angeles area, but I didn't recall ever hearing about Barstow.

"So you must have gone to the beach a lot growing up," I offered.

Grant laughed. "Barstow's in the middle of the desert. The Mojave Desert."

I didn't quite associate California with a desert landscape, although I knew there was desert in the Golden State. I still couldn't quite visualize what he was talking about.

"Have you ever heard of Las Vegas?" he asked.

"Yeah, but I've never been there."

"Well, Barstow is between Las Vegas and Los Angeles. Johnny Carson makes a lot of jokes about Barstow being in the middle of nowhere, but I think it was a great place to grow up. We'd go dirt biking in the desert, shoot jackrabbits, and go camping."

Camping? Our family's idea of roughing it was staying at Howard Johnson's. But I certainly admired anyone willing to pitch a tent and cook over a campfire.

Grant told me that he was the youngest of three children: Linda,

Greg, and then him. His parents were DeWayne and Patricia Feasel, but everyone called his mom Pat.

DeWayne had grown up in Barstow and joined the US Marine Corps during the Korean War. He wasn't an infantryman, though. The Marines recognized that DeWayne had a real talent for fixing anything because he was good with his hands, so they made him a mechanic. When he came home from the war, he put his mechanic skills to good use by working for the Santa Fe Railroad and becoming the director of maintenance for the Barstow Unified School District.

Grant's mom, Pat, used her hands in a different way: she could cook up a storm. No froufrou salads and quiche lorraine from her. With two big boys in the house and a husband who got his hands dirty during the workday, she served massive helpings of fried chicken, mashed potatoes, and homemade noodles that took her hours to prepare in the kitchen. On the sweet side, her specialties were homemade cinnamon rolls and apricot pies made from apricots that grew on a backyard tree.

Grant told me he started playing organized football when he was eight years old. His dad was the coach, and Grant said that there was nothing better than traveling to Victorville and Apple Valley and coming home with a big victory.

I asked Grant how he and his brother grew so tall. He said his dad was just six feet tall, but his mom was almost that height, so they must have taken after her. His older sister, Linda, was shorter than me, he said, and I stood at five feet seven inches.

"Did you play any other sports growing up?" I asked.

"I was on the wrestling team, and I played baseball in high school," he said. "And I love skiing at Big Bear with my friends."

"You can ski too?"

Grant didn't answer. He just grinned. I knew he had to be a really good athlete to excel at all those sports, especially football since he was on a full-ride scholarship at Abilene Christian. I asked him what it was like playing football, and he said it was a lot of work. He had to lift regularly year-round, practice several hours a day, and attend team meetings after dinner. He added that he had redshirted his freshman year, so his junior year of eligibility was coming up.

"Wait a minute. How old are you?" I asked. He sure looked like a senior to me.

"I turned twenty-one in June," he said.

So he just turned twenty-one, I thought. I had turned twenty-one the previous September, so that made me nine months older than Grant. (I would later learn that Grant was born on June 28, 1960.)

"But you graduated with the Class of '78 at Barstow High, right?" I asked, which was the year I graduated from Dallas Christian.

"Yup, sure did."

So even though we were in the same school year, Grant still had two more seasons of football left. Interesting.

It also became apparent to me that he had an incredible work ethic. Grant was working for a construction company that summer, and pounding nails under a blazing hot Texas sun wasn't for the faint of heart. His blond hair was nearly white from the outdoor exposure—just like a California surfer.

What I liked about Grant was how down-to-earth he was. He didn't put on airs. He was comfortable in his own skin, and I felt comfortable around him.

GOING STEADY

My first date with Grant gave me a spark. I was happy to get to know him, and I thought it would be fun to go out with him again.

He made me wait an entire week until he called the house again and asked me to go to a movie. Grant, as I found out on the way to the cinema, loved films. We went to see *Stripes*, a Bill Murray comedy about a guy who joins the US Army when he loses his job, his apartment, his car, and his girlfriend all in the same afternoon. After the movie, he took me back to our pink house on East North Fifteenth Street, and on the back porch, he closed his eyes and leaned close to me. Our first kiss made me feel so good, and I melted like a schoolgirl.

A few days later, we drove to Will Hair Park—or "Wild Hair Park," as the students called it—in Grant's pickup, which didn't have air-conditioning. This time, Fleetwood Mac was playing, and Stevie Nicks was singing "Dreams" and "Go Your Own Way."

We were in the midst of another hot summer day, and beads of sweat rolled down his face as we drove into the park. I was doing my best not to sweat, but the curls in my hair were straightening out. Grant apologized for the heat, but it didn't matter. I was glad to spend time with him and get to know him better. I wore purple shorts and a cute shirt for Grant, and he wore his usual Levi's, T-shirt, and flip-flops. Going out with a guy who wore flip-flops took a little getting used to, but I liked the look.

He had packed his acoustic guitar, and I brought a blanket. For the next hour, he entertained me with a mini concert in the shade. It was a major wow moment for me. Grant was quiet and soft-spoken, yet he had the self-confidence to sing in front of me—and play the guitar well. That was a beautiful moment at the start of our relationship. I had never known anyone like him.

We went out regularly after that, and as I got to know him better, I couldn't imagine going through life without him. He boosted my self-esteem by laughing at things I'd say or remarking how witty I was.

Our early dates even included going to church together. Grant wanted to show me that his faith in God was important to him, so he invited me to join him at a little country church fifteen minutes from Abilene Christian. Set in the middle of a large tumbleweed-strewn dirt lot, and with a corrugated metal roof on a plain brown stucco building, Hamby Church of Christ was where the ACU men's basketball coach, Willard Tate, preached every Sunday morning and evening.

Coach Tate could really bring it from the pulpit, and I remember being impressed that he was such a terrific speaker. I could also tell that he liked Grant, which meant that Grant was a regular at Hamby. The fact that people who mattered knew that Grant was a good guy was very appealing to me. When he introduced me to his friends, one of the first things they'd say was, "Grant is a great guy."

We'd been seeing each other pretty regularly for a month when summer training camp started in early August for the 1981 football season. Grant informed me that he wouldn't be able to see me as much as he wanted to.

"I have a heavy schedule," he said. "I'll be practicing a lot during training camp, and then during the season, I have classes in the morning and football practice in the afternoon, plus I have to get into the weight room. I also have to travel to away games while keeping up with my classes and labs."

Grant had made no bones about the fact that his studies were very important to him because he was a premed student.

I've never forgotten how he told me on our first date that he had wanted to become a dentist since he was very young. A full-ride football scholarship at Abilene Christian was a way for him to get a free undergraduate education. Although Grant was too proud to admit this, I figured out later that his parents didn't have the financial means to pay for Grant's (or Linda's or Greg's) college tuition and living expenses.

Football was Grant's ticket out of Barstow. The reason why he stayed in Abilene during the summer instead of going back home, he said, was because he was establishing Texas residency so that he could go to a dental school in Texas and pay in-state tuition when his football career was over. I could tell that he really wanted a DDS behind his name.

I had never been around someone like Grant, who was so serious about where he was going in life. I could tell that he was just as competitive for top grades as he was competitive on the line of scrimmage. But we did not share the same study habits. I went with the flow, but he meant business. That's why he told me directly but nicely: "With football and classes starting soon, I don't know how much we're going to see each other, but I do want to see you."

"I do too," I replied, even though my heart ached. I wanted to see him a lot, and I had a sneaking feeling he felt the same way about me.

My intuition soon proved to be true. When school started, Grant asked me if I could join him for dinner every evening in the school cafeteria after his busy day ended. He had morning classes and football practice every afternoon, and sometimes he'd lift after practice if he hadn't gotten into the gym early before classes started. For three years, he'd been taking the usual premed prerequisites: chemistry, biology, organic chemistry, physics, anatomy, and calculus, plus labs. He was taking more biology and anatomy classes our first fall semester together.

When it wasn't convenient to have dinner with him, I'd visit him in the school library afterward or he'd call me at the house to say hello. He studied late except for the nights before a football game, and he had good friends in the biology department who helped him out by taking notes whenever he missed a class or lab because of football.

One evening, a few months into our dating, we were studying together at Brown Library on campus. We were probably doing more flirting than studying when he stopped and scribbled a quick sentence on a piece of paper. Then he passed the note to me with the following words:

"Hey, Cyndy, I love you!"

Reading that was exciting and confirmed what I was feeling in my heart: I was falling in love with Grant.

When I said good-bye to my boyfriend that night, I thought about what our future together might look like. I decided that if I was going to hitch my wagon to anybody, I certainly wanted to travel with someone who was going places.

From what I saw, Grant Feasel was moving fast and in the right direction.

CHAPTER 3

KEEPING MY EYES ON THE CENTER

Now that Grant and I were officially boyfriend/girlfriend, I had to boost my football IQ.

I had watched plenty of football growing up, so I knew the difference between a blitz and a prevent defense. But the intricacies of the game—trap plays, pulling guards, chop blocks, and zone coverage—were still foreign to me.

Because I was interested in everything Grant did, he saw that he had a willing student eager to learn more about the game. I liked it when he "talked football," but Grant also wanted to make sure that I had a full understanding of what his role was on the field. The starting center, he said, was the focal point of the offense. When he bent over and placed his right hand on top of the football, his job was to wait until the quarterback grunted the right word to start the play. Nothing happened until he hiked the football.

Once he snapped the ball, though, it was slam or be slammed. The irresistible force meets the immovable object. In such a scenario, Grant wanted to be the one dishing out the pain. He had to have the upper hand and maintain leverage on every block. Much attention was paid to whether Grant or his defensive counterpart was "winning the line of scrimmage"—that imaginary line crossing the field, which both offensive and defensive players cannot cross until Grant snapped the ball and the play had started.

Following every game, Grant's offensive line coach would review every single play and grade him for his ability to neutralize a defensive player. Then, during the practice, Grant would work on moving laterally and vertically while maintaining power and balance. Endless drills developed his footwork, the placement of his hands, and how he finished a block.

Playing center wasn't a glory position. Even I knew that centers never get to run with the ball or catch a pass. But as Grant pointed out to me, the center touches the football more than any other position in football. Grant was the tip of the spear, which meant he was in the middle of an orchestrated chaos that ensued every time he snapped the ball. Grant's job was to stand his ground and protect the quarterback from attacking players or use his power and explosiveness to create holes in the defensive line that the running back could sprint through for long gains.

A smile came to my face whenever Grant took a piece of paper and diagrammed plays with *X*'s and *O*'s. I soaked up everything because when you like somebody, you're interested in what he's doing. The main thing that Grant wanted me to be aware of was his blocking assignments, which changed with every snap of the ball.

With a boyfriend on the team, I certainly watched more Abilene Christian football games than I had in the past. I don't think I had attended more than a handful of Wildcat games during my first three years on campus, but once Grant and I became an item, I made sure I was sitting in Shotwell Stadium's student section for every home contest. I sat with the girlfriends of players, each of us wearing our boyfriend's number on a purple Wildcat T-shirt. I couldn't have been prouder to have #51 inscribed on my back.

Once the head referee blew the starting whistle, I was into the game. I found it hard to concentrate on watching Grant after he hiked the football because I wanted to follow the ball and see how the play turned out.

I did try to keep my eyes on Grant as best as I could because he'd ask me questions after his games—questions like, "Did you see the block I made on that long touchdown run in the second quarter?" or "Do you think I was holding on our last drive?"

I usually had answers for him, but one thing I noticed about Grant was how he was knocked down on nearly every play. Centers sure took a lot of punishment, but I could tell that Grant meted out retribution as well. He was a very physical, full-out player who never held back. His towering size and lumberjack muscles were his strengths.

The best thing about watching him play at home was the tradition of families, friends, and girlfriends coming onto the field when the game was over and offering the players congratulations (if the team won) or condolences (if the team lost) before they jogged off to the showers. It felt like an honor hugging my sweaty guy! The pride I felt carried right into the school week. Just seeing him on campus wearing his purple letterman's jacket made me tingle inside.

I wanted to see every game—home and away. Abilene Christian played in the Lone Star Conference, so away games were usually within a three- to four-hour driving radius. I loved going on road trips with players' girlfriends. Our longest excursion was to Texas A&M–Kingsville, which was near the southernmost tip of Texas and a good six-hour drive from Abilene. We stayed with a girlfriend's family on the way there and the way back and had a blast, laughing and carrying on.

MEET THE PARENTS

During the 1981 season, Grant's parents made a much longer drive to see their son play. They motored 1,162 miles between Barstow and Abilene in a big pickup truck that hauled a fifth-wheel trailer on a straight shot east via Interstate 40. The trip took eighteen hours.

The first time I met DeWayne, Pat, and Grant's older sister, Linda, was inside the lobby of Grant's dorm during homecoming weekend. (Grant still lived in a dorm because Abilene Christian had a rule that if you received a full scholarship from the school, then you had to live in a university dorm.) His family was quite friendly and seemed interested in getting to know me; I'm sure they heard all about this "Dallas girl" from Grant. After the introductions were made, Pat presented me with a wooden sewing box filled with spools of thread, needles, and buttons. I was touched by the thoughtfulness of her gift, but I hadn't done much sewing. I soon learned that Pat was quite a seamstress.

The Feasels parked their trailer in a KOA campground located in a former pecan grove near the intersection of Interstate 20 and Highways 277/83/84. Grant had said his family were campers, and he was right. His parents and older sister planned to stay for ten days so they could watch Grant play in two home games.

When Pat invited me to join them for dinner, I was impressed by how she turned their campsite into an appealing place with checkered tablecloths and all the comforts of home. I'd never camped a day in my life, so I was surprised that a campground area could look so inviting.

I worried the Feasels had preconceived ideas of me being a city girl or having certain airs, but we got along great. Around a campfire, his parents regaled me with stories of Grant growing up, like the time he and his brother, Greg, were roughhousing in the living room and fell on the coffee table, breaking off all the legs, or how they spent weekends riding dirt bikes like madmen in the Mojave Desert.

As I got to know them better, DeWayne struck me as the more reserved type, and he carried the stern demeanor of a former Marine. I could tell he was a hardworking, salt-of-the-earth kind of guy. Pat was the glue that kept the family together.

One evening around the campfire, Pat recalled the first time Grant said he wanted to become a dentist. "He was eight years old, and he had gone to the dentist to get his teeth cleaned. On the ride home, he said, 'Mom, I want to be a dentist when I grow up.' We all thought he was so cute."

We shared a good laugh because what kid *wants* to become a dentist in the third grade? But Grant did, and that didn't surprise me. I had seen how single-minded and determined he was to realize his lifelong dream of making dentistry his career, and that meant working hard to earn top grades.

Here's an example. The ACU football team traveled by bus to away games, which meant that Grant had to miss Friday classes and labs since that was a travel day. Sometimes the bus didn't return until the wee hours of Sunday morning, but by later that afternoon, Grant was meeting with classmates and having them reprise the lecture and class material. He'd sit there, taking notes by hand and wanting to know every detail. Grant told me that he had to write down everything in his own hand because once he did, he remembered the material. He had a fabulous mind and was very bright. I could study for three hours and not retain the knowledge that Grant had practically memorized in thirty minutes.

I asked him about that one time. "Grant, do you have a photographic memory? Because you seem to remember everything you see!"

"I'm not sure," he replied. "All I know is that this is what I have to do to compete. It's all about having the grades and knowing the material so I can do well on the DAT and get into dental school." Grant was referring to the Dental Admission Test, a standardized test required by all dental schools. As for grades, he carried at least a 3.75 GPA in his core classes.

I was blown away by his unflinching resolve. I was barely twenty-one, a social butterfly involved with a sorority and majoring in having a good time in college. I hate to say this for my dad's sake because he invested a lot of money in my education, but I was more interested in my social life than in studying. Grant was the total opposite. He dedicated himself to being the best in the classroom and on the field.

Gee, I thought. *I've never dated anyone who knows where he's going like Grant does.* He was a serious student and was thankful he had come to Abilene with a four-year, full-ride scholarship. He wasn't going to do anything to jeopardize that, including drinking.

He had been spooked when one of his teammates joined a big group and went country dancing at a honky-tonk outside of town. There was some drinking going on, but they were just college kids having fun. No one got drunk, but Grant's teammate got stopped by the cops and ticketed with a DUI for being over the legal limit.

Next thing his teammate knew, he had lost his full-ride scholarship and ruined his future. That scared Grant, who was goal driven and knew where he wanted to go.

Grant didn't drink during the football season. That's not to say that he *never* drank alcohol. I remember him tipping a Coors Light or two the summer we met, but Grant wasn't a party guy. He didn't have time to waste on drinking and carousing, and I liked that about him.

As for me, I didn't like the taste of beer or wine. The only time I had something to drink was when we'd be at a friend's house and a blender was churning out margaritas. I was such a lightweight; I knew one margarita was my limit. As a naturally hyper person, I didn't like the way alcohol made me feel, which explains why I rarely drank. Grant didn't go for mixed drinks. I don't remember him having anything other than an occasional Coors Light in his hands. I certainly never saw him drunk. Instead of drinking, we'd entertain ourselves by using two-for-one coupons at different hamburger restaurants near campus followed by a movie at the dollar theater.

If we didn't go to the movies together, we'd drive to Lake Fort Phantom a few miles north of Abilene, where we'd park and talk about the future. Grant said he was thinking about becoming an oral surgeon, which would demand more schooling, but his plan was to start in general dentistry and see how he liked it. His biggest concern was his fingers, several of which had been broken or stepped on while playing football. He wondered if he would have the manual dexterity needed to be a great dentist.

"Then why don't you become a doctor?" I asked. Looking inside people's mouths all day long didn't sound like much fun to me.

"Being a dentist is what I've always wanted to do," he answered. "I think I'll have more of a regular life if I become a dentist. Doctors are always on call. Sure, dentists can get called in, but doctors have less control of their hours than dentists do."

Like any young couple parking at Lake Fort Phantom, we'd often have intense make-out sessions. As our love grew for each other, there was the natural urge to express that love in a physical way. Grant and I talked about that, too, which goes to show you how he thought things through better than me.

"Look, I want our relationship to be different. I've been with girls before. I don't want us to go there," he said, referring to having a sexual relationship. "I want our relationship to be something special."

I liked that Grant wanted to wait. He respected the boundaries I set in our relationship, especially after I told him that I hadn't slept with anyone. To hear him say those things lifted my admiration and strengthened my love for him. He really raised the bar.

I know he was highly regarded on the team for the way he lived out his faith. He made sure that we went to Hamby Church of Christ every Sunday morning, and he was an integral part of a team Bible study in his dorm. I had a couple of students tell me, "Hey, I wouldn't be a Christian if it wasn't for Grant."

Grant was everything I could hope for. Not only was he awesome looking, sweet, soft-spoken, and seeking God in his life, but he appreciated me for who I was. I couldn't wait to spend the rest of my life with this amazing guy.

LOOKING DOWN THE FIELD

I wasn't the only person watching Grant closely on the football field. That fall, Grant had played so well that he attracted the attention of NFL scouts.

Grant told me that NFL scouts usually didn't come to Abilene because Shotwell Stadium wasn't easy to get to. Scouts had to take a flight to DFW and then drive three hours to Abilene. I didn't know what scouting was or how the process worked, but I thought it was cool that professional football scouts thought enough of Grant's ability to come see him play. "That's awesome," I told Grant one evening after practice, although I couldn't imagine him in a Dallas Cowboy uniform any time soon. Besides, we both knew he had his mind set on becoming a dentist and having a family.

But I was excited nonetheless. I peppered Grant with questions about what NFL scouts were looking for, which he was glad to answer. I could tell he was pleased with my interest in the scouting process, because it showed him that I was a dedicated girlfriend who shared his passion for football. He saw that I was willing to love the game and be his number one fan.

Grant and the ACU football team were easy to cheer for because they had a banner year during the 1981 season, finishing the campaign with an 8–2 record. Grant got some individual recognition as well: he was named to the All Lone Star Conference first team offense as center because he dominated the offensive line. But Grant was also honored for what he did off the field: he was named All-Academic in the Lone Star Conference and was the recipient of the Outstanding Youth of the City Award in 1981.

Everything seemed to be going his way, from the football field to his premed studies to our relationship. I remember going out for a bite to eat after the last game of the 1981 season in late November. Between mouthfuls of a cheeseburger, he matter-of-factly said that I was pretty, sweet, funny, and kind. I remember him using those descriptive words. "You have everything that I'm looking for," he said. "Everything that I've been looking for in a girl. I love you, Cyndy."

I practically melted. "I love you too."

Grant flew home to Barstow for Thanksgiving. While there, he talked to his parents about marrying me. They had seen how I completed Grant—and he completed me. They saw our love for each other as well as my willingness to become part of his world of football and medicine. They liked my vivacious personality and ability to laugh—and laugh at myself. They told Grant that they thought we were a good match.

Then Grant, being traditional, called my father and asked him for my hand. Dad and Mom had gotten to know Grant during the fall. I had brought Grant home with me over Labor Day weekend just before the season started, and they had driven to Abilene to see a couple of his football games. Dad and Mom took us out after one game to a popular steak house in town called the Town Crier. Everyone liked each other. When Grant called and spoke to my father, Dad gave his permission.

Just before Christmas break and finals, Grant asked me out for dinner and a movie (of course). We had spoken of marriage and other friends getting engaged, but I was totally clueless about what would happen that night.

After the show was over, Grant drove me back to the house I was sharing with three roommates. He parked his truck in front of our house. There wasn't a soul around, and the sky was black. Twinkling stars shone in the West Texas heavens. Grant reached for a cassette tape, which he inserted into the player. A slow ballad, featuring tinkling piano music and the raspy voice of Joe Cocker, filled the cab, singing that I was so beautiful to him.

"Cyndy, will you marry me?"

My eyes immediately filled with tears. "Will I? Of course."

I fell into the arms of my Prince Charming. His soft lips fell on mine that night, the starlight reflecting in his eyes and hair. He was shy, but he was sure of himself.

Not much else was said during that special moment. Nothing else could be said.

After an appropriate moment lapsed, I kissed Grant good night. I waved as he drove off—then turned on my heels and sprinted into my house to share the news with my roommate Suzy. She was in the shower, but that didn't stop me. I burst through the bathroom door and announced, "I'm engaged to Grant!"

My future gleamed before me as the wife of Grant Feasel, DDS, along with a house in the suburbs, a white picket fence, and carpools with kids. In other words, we were headed for a normal life.

CHAPTER 4

TIME FOR A GAME PLAN

So what did our future together look like?

Getting engaged in December usually translates to a June wedding. I was due to graduate in May with my degree in elementary art education, but Grant had to stay in Abilene to play football his senior year. Well, I suppose Grant could have graduated on time if he had planned things that way, but he *wanted* to play his last season of college football. Then he'd graduate in December with a bachelor of science degree and go on to dental school. At least, that was the general contour of the plan.

Grant was pushing for a summer wedding, but with everything on my plate—a May commencement, wedding preparations, and job seeking—my parents and I agreed that too much was up in the air. Plus, as my parents pointed out, we'd only known each other five months when Grant proposed. They counseled a longer engagement. "You don't want to rush into marriage," Dad said.

Since a summer wedding was out and Grant was playing football in the fall and finishing up with a few classes, that meant looking at a date following his graduation in mid-December. We didn't want to wait more than a year to get married since we weren't living together before the nuptials. I suggested a Christmas Eve wedding, but my family overruled that idea, as well as New Year's Eve. Then we zeroed in on the first available Saturday in January—January 8. That date stuck.

Grant didn't have an engagement ring when he asked me to marry him. He hadn't had time to shop, plus he figured that I wanted some input on the ring. Shortly after the proposal, we drove 165 miles to Lubbock because we had a school friend, Lisa Meyers, whose family owned a jewelry store.

The spring months passed quickly. My biggest worry wasn't the wedding but getting a job after I graduated since I would be the main breadwinner when we became husband and wife. I had no problem working full-time to help put Grant through dental school. It would be a team effort, although we'd have to live on my meager teacher's salary.

I did some student teaching during my last semester and had a successful experience, so I set my sights on becoming a schoolteacher. My faculty supervisor said I was a natural with kids and offered to give me a glowing recommendation to the Abilene Independent School District.

On graduation day, I walked with my class while Grant sat next to my extended family inside Moody Coliseum. My parents could tell how on-track he was about becoming a dentist and having a career that would support their daughter and a family. Grant described how he was planning to work for a dental lab during the summer—instead of pounding nails on a construction site—so he could get some experience in the medical field.

I lived in the same house with my roommates that summer and did odd jobs while I waited to hear from the Abilene school superintendent. There was no such thing as e-mail back then, but there was a phone. I must have called the superintendent every few days, inquiring if a teaching position had opened up. "I had a great student-teaching experience, and I want to stay in Abilene," I said each time we talked.

I could tell the superintendent liked my energy and enthusiasm; otherwise, he never would have taken my calls. "If there's an opening, do you care what school it is?" he asked one day.

Of course I said no. I had done some teacher aide work in various parts of town, so I figured he was referring to elementary schools situated in low-income areas. One week before the first school bell, he called and offered me a first-grade teaching position in one of the less-privileged neighborhoods.

Grant had a good experience at the dental lab where he worked making crowns and bridges. The manual dexterity needed to grip and shape crowns as well as work in close quarters inside the mouth was a huge concern to Grant because of his damaged fingers from football, but as he'd learned on the football field, practice makes perfect. Part of the Dental Admission Test that he planned to take after graduation included a manual dexterity test. Grant said that could be the most difficult part of the entrance exam for him because he felt like he knew the human physiology material.

Before we knew it, summer camp opened for the 1982 Wildcats football season. Big things were expected from Grant for his senior year. He had been elected one of four team captains, following in the footsteps of his brother, Greg, who was a team captain in 1979. In his "spare" time, Grant volunteered to speak at high schools and in front of prep football teams on behalf of the Fellowship of Christian Athletes, encouraging younger students to "get into the game" when it came to taking their Christian faith to the next level.

Practice, weight training, team meetings, classwork, outside speaking, and studying, studying, studying didn't leave much alone time for us, but I understood that our hectic schedule was for a season. As for me, I was teaching first grade five days a week and preparing class lessons in the evenings. At a minimum, Grant and I made sure we ate dinner together every night, usually inside the school cafeteria.

Talking about our upcoming wedding gave us a welcome respite from our busy lives. Once we were married, we told ourselves, things would settle down.

We'd have more time for each other, right?

CLEARING THE COBWEBS

Abilene Christian didn't put the same powerhouse team on the field as the year before, but everyone said Grant was a star center that defenses had to take into account.

He played every down on offense, as well as on the punt team and field goal unit since he was the deep snapper. He never got injured, although he admitted to feeling aches and pains after games.

At one home game midway through the season, though, I noticed Grant wasn't in the game to snap the ball to the quarterback. I searched the sidelines and found my fiancé sitting on the bench, hunched over. A couple of trainers were gathered around him, and one had his hand on Grant's shoulder pads while he waved something under Grant's nose.

And just like that, Grant stood up, put his helmet back on, and jogged back onto the field. My eyes followed #51 as he took his place in the team huddle.

"What was that all about?" I asked Grant later that night. "Why were you pulled out?"

"I had a concussion," he said.

I didn't know about concussions in football. Nobody talked about them back then. I knew concussions were serious because my younger sister Lori, five years old at the time, had fallen and cracked her head on the concrete floor of our garage. Lori spent seven days in the hospital with a concussion and cracked skull. So when I heard Grant mention that he had a concussion, I envisioned some sort of skull fracture.

"Why did you go back into the game if you had a concussion?" I asked. A head injury is serious.

"Oh, they just gave me some smelling salts on the sidelines."

"Smelling salts? What are those?"

"It's a small packet of ammonium carbonate," Grant explained. "One of the trainers broke open a packet and held it under my nose. The ammonia gas was really strong and irritated my nostril membranes and lungs. I was fine after that. The smelling salts cleared up everything in a hurry."

"Just like that you were okay?"

Grant shrugged his massive shoulders. "Yeah, I was good to go. I wanted to get back into the game to help my team."

Grant had another reason to stay in the game: NFL scouts were watching him from the grandstands with clipboards in hand. Word was getting around the NFL coaching circles that Grant was a force to be reckoned with. As I later heard it said, you can't coach for size; and Grant had the height and strength that NFL coaches appreciated. No center had ever played the position at six feet seven inches tall.

The NFL scouts were not only coming to the games, but they were attending practices as well to get a closer look at Grant. All this attention got my fiancé thinking: *Can I play in the NFL?*

It was fun batting around that question over dinner together, but the idea of Grant playing professional football seemed awfully remote. Abilene Christian had just moved up from NAIA Division I to NCAA Division II with the 1982 season, but even then, there was a huge gap between the Abilene Christians of the football world and major football powers like the University of Texas and University of Oklahoma. That's why very few ACU players had ever made it to the NFL and why no player had been drafted in six years—and that was back in the day when the NFL Draft was twelve rounds!

The Wildcats finished with a solid 6–4–1 record, and Grant swept up all sorts of accolades, including being named to three All-America teams for Division II:

- first team Kodak All-America
- first team Associated Press All-America
- second team Academic All-America

Grant was also named first team All Lone Star Conference and LSC Offensive Lineman of the Year. When Grant learned his picture would be placed in Moody Coliseum with the other All-American Wildcats, including his brother, Greg, he told a reporter, "We're the first two brothers to get our pictures up there. My parents are really proud, and it means a lot to me because it means so much to them."

EXCHANGING VOWS

We had a big wedding—mainly because the invitation list was filled with my parents' friends or business associates. The Barstow contingent consisted of Grant's immediate family. Mom organized everything and had such a good time that she started her own wedding planning business afterward.

Around five hundred people filled my home church, Saturn Road Church of Christ, for the Saturday night ceremony. Dad walked me down the aisle to the front of the sanctuary, where Ray Hawkins, a good family friend and a minister, was waiting. "Who gives this woman to be married to this man?" he asked with a familiar smile.

"Her mother and I do," Dad replied. Then Dad stepped up and took Ray's spot so that he could officiate the wedding. (My father was licensed to marry couples in the state of Texas and had married family members in the past.)

Dad led us through our wedding vows and the exchange of rings. As I felt Grant's huge hands holding mine, I thought he would be holding me the rest of our lives. After Dad pronounced us husband and wife, Grant leaned forward and kissed me full on the lips, and I felt a rush of electricity.

A punch-and-cake reception was held in the church fellowship hall. No alcohol was served since we were in a church setting. The reception lasted a long time, and by the time Grant and I checked into our honeymoon suite at the Hyatt Regency in downtown Dallas at midnight, we were exhausted.

We were also excited since it was our first night together. On our king-size bed were rose petals, a box of chocolates, and a cheese-and-fruit basket. We were famished and devoured the chocolates in a spasm of laughter.

On a nearby table, a bottle of French champagne lay in a bucket of ice.

"What do you think of cracking open that champagne?" Grant asked as he slipped off the jacket of his cream-colored tux.

"Yes, let's have some. I've never had champagne before," I said.

"Me neither. I guess there's a first time for everything," he said with a gleam in his eye.

Grant had never opened a bottle of champagne before either. It took him awhile to work the cork when . . . explosion! The cork shot across the room, which we thought was the funniest thing ever.

And that's how we toasted the start of our physical relationship together. We weren't nervous at all. We were happy and thrilled. It was sweet. It was tender. It was kind. It was easy . . . just like Grant—easygoing.

And then we both fell asleep. I think I anticipated that we would make love all night like they do in romance novels, but we were both too exhausted to continue. We slept in and got up in the morning and drove five hours to San Antonio, where we checked into a nice hotel near the River Walk, a popular place for honeymooning couples in Texas. After two nights in San Antonio, we traveled back to Abilene on Tuesday afternoon because I couldn't miss more than two days of school.

Grant moved into a one-bedroom apartment that I had taken a month before we got married. I had no complaints about married life. We laughed. We had fun. We were husband and wife.

Grant was calming while I was high-strung. I went like a jackrabbit from one thing to the next. Grant was soothing and in control. He made me a better person, and he liked being with me because I lifted him up.

I couldn't believe how organized he was. He hung his clothes in perfect order in our closet—and by color . . . blues with blues, whites with whites, and purples with purples (the ACU colors). His underwear and socks were folded a certain way. He'd put his notebooks and school supplies in his backpack every night so that the next morning he would be ready. He was that kind of guy—a neat freak. Nothing was left out. Everything was packed away. No messes.

Me? I'd be scrambling to find my car keys in the morning so I wouldn't be late for my first-grade class. "Where are my car keys? Have you seen my keys?" I'd say frantically as the minutes counted down.

We had a bar area connected to the kitchen, where he studied. His books were stacked in the same place every day so that he knew exactly where everything was. Notepads were atop books, and pens and pencils filled a mug.

Grant was driven and determined, the most focused person I'd ever met. I admired those qualities in him and completely trusted him to do what he said he was going to do. I felt safe with Grant. He would protect me. He said so in his wedding vows.

In our first couple of months of married life, Grant spent most of his time studying for the DAT exam given in March. He also found time to lift at the ACU weight room as part of his preparation for the NFL Draft in late April, but his studies had priority. The National Invitational Camp, the forerunner to the NFL Combine, was held in Tampa, Florida, but Grant wasn't asked to participate.

Grant's studies paid off, and he scored well on the DAT. By early April, we found out that he had been accepted to Texas' three dental schools in Dallas, Houston, and Galveston. He visited them all and decided that he would attend the Texas A&M University Baylor College of Dentistry in Dallas, a perfect fit since that would place us in close proximity to my parents and sisters.

Maybe we'll end up in the Big D when Grant goes into practice, I daydreamed.

It sure seemed possible.

DRAFT DAY

We talked about Grant playing in the pros. He told me that he wouldn't try out as a free agent, but if he got drafted, then he wanted to give the NFL a shot.

"I can go to dental school anytime, but I will only have the opportunity to play in the NFL one time," he said over hamburgers one night. His acceptance by the Baylor College of Dentistry was good for two years, so if he tried to make an NFL team and came up short, then he could step right back onto the dental track.

I wasn't thinking about the NFL as much as Grant was. I didn't know that much about the NFL Draft or understand how professional football worked. I knew players were on teams, but I didn't know how they got there.

As far as Grant was concerned, he was in a win-win situation. If he got drafted, then he could try to make the team. If he got passed over, then football would be in his rearview mirror and he'd enroll at the Baylor College of Dentistry.

The NFL Draft wasn't a big deal in the spring of 1983. On Tuesday morning, April 26, before I left for Bonham Elementary, Grant explained how teams took turns picking players coming out of college. "I don't think I'll be taken in the first three rounds," he said. "We'll just have to see."

I kissed Grant good-bye. He looked relaxed about the whole thing. All he could do was hang out at our apartment and wait for the phone to ring in those pre–cell phone days.

When I came home from school that afternoon, the first thing I said was, "Did anyone call?"

"Haven't heard anything yet," Grant replied. At dinnertime, the phone still hadn't stirred. We decided to go out and get a hamburger. We were just about to leave the apartment when the phone jangled.

Grant listened for a moment and then said, "Thanks, Coach, I'm really excited." Then he listened a bit longer and thanked the coach for the call, telling him that he wouldn't be disappointed.

When he hung up, Grant looked at me. "That was the head coach of the Baltimore Colts. His name is Frank Kush. He called to congratulate me on being selected in the sixth round by the Colts and to get ready to report to training camp."

"When does that start?"

"The middle of July."

"Did he tell you where?"

"At some college in Maryland."

"You want to go, don't you?"

Grant drew me close. "Listen, ever since I started playing football at age eight, it's been my dream to play in the NFL. Every kid has that dream. And now I have a once-in-a-lifetime chance. I have to take a shot at it."

I squeezed Grant. "I'm happy for you—for us," I said. Even though dental school was exciting, I was just as thrilled about this opportunity as Grant was. The last thing I wanted to do was hold him back from fulfilling his dream.

CHAPTER 5

AN NFL TRYOUT

Three weeks after the NFL draft, in the middle of May, Grant flew to Baltimore for rookie minicamp. We would not see each other for the next three-and-a-half months, since after minicamp was over Grant would stay in Baltimore to work out at the team facilities, watch game film, and be tutored by the coaches on the intricacies of the Colts' playbook. There was a lot to learn, and remaining in Baltimore was the best way for Grant to show his coaches how much he wanted to play professional football.

Sixth-round draft choices usually don't stick in the NFL, but Grant was optimistic because the Colts' coaching staff led him to believe that he would make the team. He said it didn't make financial sense to fly me out to Baltimore and get a short-term apartment and then turn around and move back to Texas if he got cut. Grant wanted everything done in the right order, which meant his being 100 percent focused on making the team and *then* bringing me out to the East Coast.

Grant suggested that I stay with my parents until things got sorted out. He thought Garland would be the most loving, safest place for me, which was so Grant. Being separated from my husband and sleeping alone in my old bedroom, however, was not exactly how I imagined life as a newlywed, but that's what we had to do. I decided to take two summer school classes, which kept me busy and occupied.

Communication with Grant was sporadic since we could only talk on the phone every two or three days, but every time he would tell me, "It looks good." But he also made this telling observation: "Everyone's huge here. There are a lot of big guys, and they all come from big schools." Grant definitely felt like an underdog and wondered if he was too skinny for the pros.

Grant worked his tail off at training camp and showed the Colts' coaching staff the outsized work ethic that had brought him that far. He was always one of the first to arrive at the team training facility and one of the last to leave, a practice that would stay with him until his last day in the NFL. Grant knew he had to work extra hard from sunup to sundown because the bar was raised so high in this physically demanding sport. Each NFL player was an exceptional athlete, but Grant worried that he didn't have the raw athletic ability that professional football demanded.

We also talked about the big picture. Grant believed that God was leading him to the NFL, and I agreed with him. I told him that he'd done an awesome job of being a positive example at Abilene Christian, and there was no reason why he couldn't be a ray of light in an NFL locker room.

When training camp started the third week of July at Goucher College in Towson, Maryland, Grant did whatever it took to get noticed. I heard from him less because he had to stand in line to use the only pay phone in the dorm hallway. Under those circumstances, we didn't have any heart-to-heart discussions—or very long ones. Each time we talked, though, he remained hopeful that he'd make the Colts' roster.

As training camp progressed, he passed the first cut, followed by the second, and then a week before the start of the 1983 season, Grant received the welcome news that he had made the fifty-three-man roster, backing up center Ray Donaldson and playing on special teams—mainly on the kickoff coverage unit.

Grant was absolutely thrilled to be part of the NFL, the culmination of a dream that had started on rocky lawns in the middle of the Mojave Desert. He had reached the pinnacle of the most popular sport in America—pro football. I was proud of him, as were his parents.

I flew to Baltimore, and we moved into a beautiful, brand-new apartment in Reisterstown, Maryland, a half hour northwest of Baltimore but close to the team's training complex in Owings Mills. Disappointingly, I did not see Grant very much. Playing professional football was a seven-day-a-week endeavor. Tuesdays were Grant's day off, but he usually spent the morning at the team facility getting his body worked on for one reason or another. Our only "couple time" was on Tuesday afternoons when we hung out at the apartment or did errands together. The social highlight of the week was going out to dinner on Tuesday nights with Christian teammates and friends like Jeff and Sheryl Jaros. Other than that, it was football 24-7 for Grant.

Another couple we immediately bonded with was Leo and Cindy Wisniewski. Leo was the Colts' starting nose guard, so he and Grant butted heads all afternoon on the practice field since Grant played center on the "scout" team, which was the second-string offense. The Wisniewskis were a fabulous Christian couple, so it didn't surprise me that Leo went into the ministry when his playing days were over. (Today, Leo is the director of Locking Arms Men, a men's outreach in the Pittsburgh area.)

Weekends were tough, too, since once Grant left our apartment on Saturday morning, I didn't see him again until Sunday night. The Colts team stayed at a downtown hotel on the eve of home games or boarded a charter flight for a Saturday night stay in another city and a road game Sunday afternoon. Sometimes the team didn't return until the wee hours of Monday morning.

Home or away, I went to church alone on Sunday mornings. I found a good Church of Christ congregation that I liked, but it takes a while to get to know people in a new church. I spent my days exploring Baltimore and getting to know the city. I visited art museums, the vibrant waterfront, historic ships moored within the Inner Harbor, and Fort McHenry, the birthplace of "The Star-Spangled Banner," our national anthem. I checked out stacks of books from the local library. I painted and sewed. I drove ninety minutes to the Amish country outside of Lancaster, Pennsylvania.

I was also a little Betty Crocker, cooking up a storm so that Grant would have a great-tasting, hot meal waiting for him when he arrived at the apartment at 7:00 p.m. each night. I was always excited to see him. I usually had to carry the conversation while we ate, however, because he was exhausted from his physical labors. It became apparent that Grant gave his best hours of the day at the office—the NFL practice field. He was really tired when he came home and often complained about aches and pains in his neck and lower back.

"How come you're hurting?" I asked one evening. "Isn't practice supposed to be easier than playing the games?"

"You can't lie back," he said. "I have to give everything I've got in practice because you never know when your situation could change."

That's how Grant looked at practice. He wanted to make a strong impression on his coaches so that they'd send him in, and once in the game, he'd show his coaches and teammates that they could count on him. "That's why I always have to be ready," Grant said.

After I'd clear the dinner dishes, he'd relax in the easy chair in front of the TV—and quickly fall into a deep sleep. I'd tap him on the shoulder and trundle him off to bed. This happened nearly every night.

That was another adjustment I had to make—a slim-pickings love life. I thought there would be more action on that front, especially since we had to forgo making love during the three-and-a-half-month separation, but Grant was too tired to be physically intimate on many evenings.

The first nine months of our marriage:

- I didn't see my husband much.
- I was in a city in which I knew no one.

- I was lonely and missed my family back in Dallas.
- My newlywed husband was too bone-tired to initiate sex much of the time.

After a month in Baltimore, I started sleeping in until noon, which was very uncharacteristic of me. After Grant fell asleep in his easy chair and I helped him to bed, I would stay up and watch several TV shows until eleven o'clock or so to keep myself company. Then I'd tiptoe into our bedroom, careful not to wake him up since he needed plenty of rejuvenating rest.

There were times when Grant would come home at lunchtime to check up on me, and I would still be in bed. That was a ridiculous way to live. I should have been up and busy, but I felt like I didn't have anything to get up for.

Meanwhile, Grant was dealing with his own frustrations. His coach, Frank Kush, was an old-school disciplinarian who yelled and screamed at his players and liked to say that he treated everyone the same way—badly. Grant didn't like being browbeaten at practice, but he had to take it since he was fighting to keep his roster spot. On Sundays, Grant was relegated to special teams and never snapped the ball during his rookie year. Grant wanted to play more and told me so—dumping his frustrations on me since he could never say anything to Coach Kush or the rest of the coaching staff. Grant wasn't fulfilled practicing and not playing because he was an overachiever. He wanted to be an integral part of the team.

Although my husband wasn't getting his uniform dirty on Sunday afternoons, I enjoyed going to the Colts' football games. Sitting inside aging Memorial Stadium was a lot different from watching games at Abilene Christian, however. Known as "The World's Largest Outdoor Insane Asylum," Memorial Stadium attracted a boisterous, blue-collar crowd. I'd never been to a game where everyone drank a ton of beer and yelled at the players and the refs at the top of their lungs. At Dallas

Cowboys games, people dressed up nicely and cheered on their Cowboys, but in Baltimore the grandstands were filled with loud, rowdy fans, which was something I wasn't used to.

That doesn't mean I didn't enjoy going to Grant's games or being an NFL wife. I never wondered, *What am I doing here?* or thought, *I wish we were home.* I reminded myself that I was part of an adventure that few get to experience.

But I wondered why I slept until the crack of noon on many days.

SETTING DOWN ROOTS

We didn't stay in Baltimore for the off-season.

Now that we had a little money in the bank, Grant and I talked about buying a house in the Dallas Metroplex. I loved the idea of having our own home because I wanted a place to come back to. Both Grant and I were aware that NFL careers were notoriously short.

Grant received a $50,000 signing bonus and was paid around $70,000 in salary, which amounts to around $120,000 and $170,000 in today's dollars, respectively. That's a lot less money than what today's NFL players command, but back then, especially for a twenty-three-year-old fresh out of college, we were able to make some serious bank deposits and pay off our wedding rings.

Grant was very careful about how we spent our money. His agent invested most of his signing bonus into various land deals, and what was left over from his NFL paycheck went straight into our savings account. (NFL players are paid one-seventeenth of their annual salary after every game and the bye week.)

We decided to look for a home in Rowlett, five miles east of my parents' place in pricier Garland. While house hunting, Grant said, "We're not going to overextend ourselves. We're not going to go crazy and buy a big expensive house like a lot of professional athletes do."

We purchased a home for considerably less than what we could afford—a three-bedroom, two-thousand-square-foot ranch house for around $150,000, if memory serves. I was absolutely delighted with our new home and the location close to family.

We'd been in our new home for only a month when we heard stunning news out of Baltimore: after years of unsuccessfully lobbying for a new stadium to replace a deteriorating Memorial Stadium, the Colts organization packed up a fleet of Mayflower moving vans and relocated to Indianapolis in the dead of night on March 29, 1984.

Grant and I shrugged our shoulders. A franchise relocation was out of our control. Now we would be embarking on another adventure to a region of the country that neither of us had ever visited.

Grant remained the backup center and had to endure another ration of verbal abuse from Coach Kush, who ruled the practice field with an iron fist. One of Kush's favorite drills was called Bull in the Ring. Players would form a circle, and then Kush would call out a player that he wanted to pick on to stand in the middle of the circle. Then the coach would bark out a uniform number, and that player had to charge the player standing in the middle of the circle. They would try to knock each other to the ground, delivering body blows until Kush's whistle blew, at which time the player giving the best effort got to return to the circle. Then the "motivational" drill started all over again.

The Colts' inaugural season in Indianapolis was rolling along when suddenly my husband was put on waivers to clear a roster spot for another player. In other words, the Colts felt Grant was expendable and let him go after six games. We were dealing with the shock and disappointment of that decision when suddenly—just a few hours later—the Minnesota Vikings claimed Grant off the waiver wire, saying they wanted him. Now we were overjoyed.

We immediately packed our suitcases, tossed the rest of our belongings into our Chevy Blazer, and got on the road to Minneapolis. Time for another interesting experience.

Getting cut made Grant nervous, however, since he felt he had to prove himself all over again to new coaching staff. He also felt the pressure of owning a home back in Dallas. Once we arrived in Minnesota his attitude brightened because he saw his first playing time and was called upon to perform the deep snapping on punts, field goals, and extra points. The head coach, Les Steckel, who would later become the president and CEO of Fellowship of Christian Athletes in 2005, was much more nurturing.

Minnesota was where I heard, for the first time, Grant saying things like "I got my bell rung" after a game or "I suffered a stinger" in practice. His body took a lot more abuse, and I noticed that he was staying longer after practice to get iced and sit in whirlpool baths.

Unfortunately, the Vikings finished last in the National Football Conference's "Black and Blue" division with a 3–13 record, and Coach Steckel was fired. Longtime Minnesota coach Bud Grant agreed to return after a one-year hiatus for his eighteenth season as the Vikings coach.

IN A FAMILY WAY

What I remember most about the 1984 season is that I stopped taking my birth control pills. I didn't like the way my body reacted to oral contraceptives, and it seemed like there was a baby boom among the Viking wives. I started thinking, *Why don't we start a family?* We had been married a year, and I always had wanted to be a mother.

So one night—it must have been a Monday night before his off day—I said to Grant, "I don't want to take my birth control pills any longer. Why don't we give things a try and see what happens?"

The "trying" part didn't happen as often as I hoped, and I didn't get pregnant in Minnesota. We returned to our Rowlett home when the season was over, and in late January 1985, we flew out to California to see Grant's parents. While there, we drove to nearby Big Bear for a weekend of skiing.

These days, NFL contracts routinely forbid risky endeavors like snow skiing, cliff diving, and riding a motorcycle, but back then, Grant could do what he wanted during the off-season. When he said he wanted to take me skiing, I didn't bat an eye. From the stories his parents told me, I knew Grant was a fabulous skier. He convinced me that we'd have a great time at Snow Summit, one of the Big Bear ski resorts.

After a day of skiing—or rather, after a day of Grant skiing and me mainly riding the bunny lift—we told funny stories about ourselves at a lovely restaurant in Big Bear, and then we returned to an A-frame cabin we had rented in the woods. Grant made a fire in the bedroom's stone fireplace and turned out the lights. We took our fill of love, and afterward I thought, *I just got pregnant.* Within a few weeks, we knew for sure. Grant and I would become parents, and our fathers and mothers would become grandparents for the first time. This was big news.

I think the reality of the pregnancy caught Grant flatfooted, however, when he did the math: a late January pregnancy meant a late September delivery. He would be becoming a dad at the start of the 1985 NFL season! He didn't say anything, but I could see it written all over his face: *The baby conflicts with football!*

I didn't have an easy pregnancy. I couldn't eat anything, and what food I managed to get down didn't stay long in my stomach. I threw up for sixteen weeks and lost so many nutrients that there were occasions when my ob-gyn administered an IV to restore fluids and nutrients to my body.

I wasn't easy to live with either. Cranky and out of sorts, I didn't sleep well and complained about being tired all the time. As the start of training camp at Minnesota State University in Mankato loomed, we agreed that it was best for me to stay home and have the baby in Rowlett. Grant promised to leave the team when I went into labor.

My husband flew to Minnesota carrying a folder that contained his goals for the 1985 season. Grant—always the planner—had written down a list of his objectives on a three-by-five card and tucked it into his Bible with the following heading:

Training Camp Goals for Vikings 1985

- Be Tough
- Don't Be Hurt
- Don't Get Tired or Dizzy
- Do It for Cyndy & the Baby

Grant was dedicated to the NFL and took his job very seriously. His teammates gave him the nickname "Fighting Feasel" because of his many altercations with defensive players during practice. Grant didn't take crap from anyone. Every day—every play—was intense. That's how he rolled. He didn't want anything distracting him or taking away his focus.

I remember one particular phone call from the dorms at Minnesota State that sticks with me to this day. "You know, I'm having a hard time in training camp because I'm worried about you and the baby, and that takes my mind off of concentration," he said.

Grant shared this thought more than once with me. He wasn't being mean or cavalier about my condition. It's just that he was so motivated to do his best that he didn't want to siphon off any mental energy from the task at hand—playing football—by worrying about our unborn baby and me.

He would soon have a lot to worry about.

CHAPTER 6

A CHARGED TIME-OUT

On a hot summer afternoon in 1985 on a collegiate football field in Minnesota, Grant hiked the ball to quarterback Wade Wilson and immediately looked to neutralize the nose tackle. Grant was in the final five minutes of the last two-a-day practice for the Minnesota Vikings training camp that year.

It was the start of another offensive play—something Grant had done thousands of times since he began playing organized football in Barstow. Grant knew that once he snapped the ball, bodies would be flying everywhere and that he could count on a violent collision between him and a defensive lineman.

Grant was used to physical mayhem occurring every time the pigskin left his hands. He operated in a savage environment where linemen on both sides of the ball slammed into each other at full force in order to gain a competitive advantage.

As the center, Grant anchored the line of scrimmage and used his peripheral vision to keep track of how the defensive players were reacting to the moves made by the players on offense. If a running play had been called, Grant shoved his defensive counterpart in a certain direction to create a gap in the offensive line so the halfback could "run for daylight." If a pass play was called, then Grant dropped back two steps and was the center point of the "pocket" of protection for the quarterback. Grant was always looking to his right or left—as well as straight ahead—to pick up a charging defensive player. In football they call it "keeping your head on a swivel."

I don't know if a passing or a running play had been called on that hot summer afternoon in Minnesota when Grant snapped the ball and a ballet of chaos ensued between the offense and defense. All I know is that a member of the Minnesota Vikings defensive line—probably weighing 285 pounds or more—crashed into Grant's left knee and shredded his ACL (anterior cruciate ligament), MCL (medial collateral ligament), and meniscus. Grant screamed in agony and dropped like a felled oak. Whistles blew, and action stopped. His left knee was wrecked beyond comprehension.

I was in Dallas when I got the call from a member of the Vikings organization informing me that Grant had been severely injured at training camp. This happened in mid-August, during my eighth month of pregnancy. The Vikings team doctor examined Grant and scheduled him for reconstructive surgery the next day to repair his ACL, MCL, and torn meniscus, which had practically exploded in the pileup of bodies.

My knees got weak when I greeted Grant at DFW Airport a few days later. A white cast ran the length of his left leg from his hip to his toes. My six-foot, seven-inch husband wasn't very agile on a pair of "tall man" crutches.

Grant, understandably, was in a distant mood. While on the drive to our Rowlett home, he told me, "I think the reason I got hurt was because I wasn't completely concentrating on what I should have been concentrating on."

His words didn't strike me back then as they do today, but looking back, this was my first clue that Grant was taking football so seriously that he didn't want to think about anything else—including the imminent birth of his first child. In a way, I think he was indirectly blaming me for the unfortunate injury because he believed that he had let his concentration wander for a split second because he had too much on his mind. Otherwise, he might have picked up the presence of the other player—and reacted in time—and prevented the collision that tore up the inner workings of his left knee.

I saw the injury in a different light. While it was horrible news to hear that Grant would miss the entire 1985 season, the silver lining was he'd be home with me for the birth of the baby and be able to bond with our first child. I was also relieved to learn that since Grant was injured in training camp, the Vikings were obligated to pay his contracted salary in full.

I had finally started to feel better several weeks before my due date when I suddenly began leaking amniotic fluid that protected the unborn baby inside the womb. My ob-gyn was concerned enough to recommend that we induce labor.

If I had known that using Pitocin to spur contractions—instead of waiting a bit longer for nature to run its course—would result in such a painful delivery, I would have gladly waited. Instead, I endured hard labor while my medical team worked to bring a baby boy into the world during the early morning hours of September 25, 1985.

Grant, wearing long purple shorts with a Minnesota Vikings logo, hobbled around the delivery room at Presbyterian Hospital of Dallas on crutches. He was extremely happy to become a father, and we named our son Sean Geoffrey Feasel. The name Sean was Grant's idea. My husband loved James Bond movies, so he thought Sean would be a cool name. Geoffrey was simply a name we liked.

Sean wasn't an easy baby. He cried a lot and was hard to soothe, which affected Grant's sleep—and tempered his eagerness to have another child right away. A couple of months after Sean's birth, he told me, "We're going back on birth control because we don't need another kid right now."

During our dating days, Grant had said he wanted four children, but after he saw how much work was involved in caring for an infant, he wanted to slow down the train. Grant took having children very seriously and was also concerned about the financial implications of having another child with his football career on hiatus. Six months after Sean's birth, I broached the topic of having more children again. "Not while I'm coming back from knee surgery," Grant said. "There's too much in the air."

Grant's mind was set on getting back to the NFL.

ON THE SIDELINES

I enjoyed watching NFL games on TV with Grant. Not only did this give me the opportunity to be part of his world, but it made me feel connected to him. Asking "inside football" questions about the quarterback's cadence or why offensive linemen double-teamed certain players was a nice way to spend an afternoon or evening together. Grant's eyes lit up and his voice became animated when we started talking football.

On November 18, 1985, we were watching a *Monday Night Football* game between the Washington Redskins and New York Giants. Joe Theismann, the Redskins quarterback, was hit by Giants linebacker Lawrence Taylor. Two major bones below Theismann's knee snapped, and one jutted through the skin—on live television. Grant turned pale as he watched.

"You can quit this football," I said. "Let's go to dental school! I can go back to work, and my mom and dad can look after Sean while you're taking classes and I'm teaching in the classroom." I kept going.

"You've been severely injured, and I don't want you getting hurt any-more. It's upsetting to me. You've been in a cast for months. If you play again, the chances of your knee getting torn up again are pretty high because of the position you play. I want Sean to stay here in Rowlett, not live in some apartment in Minneapolis. If you go to dental school and we have to sell this house and live in a dinky apartment somewhere, that's fine by me. We'll make it work."

Grant shook his head. "I don't want to do that. I want to give football another shot. I didn't try long enough. Sorry, but I feel strongly about this."

After nearly two years of marriage, I had learned that when Grant had his mind made up to do something, then nobody could get in the way. He was sweet, tender, and kind, but underneath that peaceful, easy feeling was a layer of steely toughness. He knew what he wanted to do and the direction he was going.

That was the end of our discussion.

Sometime in early December, Grant flew back to the Vikings team facility in suburban Eden Prairie, Minnesota, where the doctors who'd performed the reconstructive surgery on Grant's knee removed the cast and checked on the healing process. He was cleared to start rehabbing the knee once he returned to Texas.

Grant's left leg was stiff and sore when the cast came off, but he was more concerned about losing so much weight. Any bulk in his body was gone, and he looked downright skinny. Opposing defenses could push a lighter Grant Feasel around with ease.

Grant drove to a health food store and bought big tubs of powdered protein to mix into thrice-daily shakes. Then he asked me to make him high-calorie meals with plenty of starches: spaghetti, lasagna, mashed potatoes, rice, and dinner rolls. Then after polishing off seconds and thirds, he filled a bowl with a monster-sized portion of fudge ripple ice cream. I couldn't keep enough half gallons of the vanilla-and-chocolate-swirl ice cream in the freezer.

During the spring of 1986, I noticed that Grant had his nose buried in a book entitled *Kaplan MCAT Practice Tests*.

"What's MCAT?" I asked. "Something to do with dentistry?"

"MCAT stands for Medical College Admission Test. I'm thinking that maybe I could become a doctor."

"A doctor? I thought football was more—"

"I haven't changed my mind about football. But if my knee doesn't respond, I want to have options. I'm thinking about becoming a doctor because dentists have to stand a lot of hours and do a lot of leaning over. I'm not sure my back can take that any longer—or my neck."

"Because of football," I said.

"Right."

Looking back at this conversation, what Grant was saying was that football had already exacted a huge physical toll on his twenty-five-year-old body. Years of bending over to hike the ball and getting slammed after the snap had left him with a continually sore back and neck. I noticed that every time Grant drove, he couldn't fully turn his head to see if there were any cars in his blind spot. He also complained that his battered fingers and scraped knuckles were worse than ever.

"Maybe I could become a doctor if football doesn't work out," Grant continued. "I can't become a surgeon because they have to stand all day, but maybe I can see patients instead."

I welcomed this sort of thinking and told Grant that if he decided to become a doctor, then he'd become the best doctor in the whole wide world. For the next month, Grant planted his nose in the Kaplan test preparation books. "I wanna blow the top off the MCAT," he said.

I believed him. Grant still had an amazing ability to read something once or twice and retain all that information.

And that's exactly what happened when he took the Medical College Acceptance Test. Grant did well, which raised his confidence about the future. "This is a really good option for me because I'd rather go to medical school than dental school," he said.

Grant applied to every medical school in Texas and was accepted into every one. The University of Texas Southwestern Medical School in Dallas, which Grant wanted to attend, gave him a deferral.

"Sure, we can wait for you," the adviser said. "You just let us know when you're ready."

A LONGER TIME-OUT

Grant continued to work hard to get himself ready to play football again.

We moved into an apartment in Minneapolis right before the start of the 1986 training camp, but Grant was worried that his left knee wouldn't withstand the rigors demanded on the line of scrimmage.

His doubts were confirmed when Vikings team doctors put his knee through a battery of tests—and he flunked. But the Vikings organization wanted him to keep rehabbing the knee with the idea that they would activate Grant sometime during the 1986 season. This was great news since their decision meant that Grant remained on the Vikings payroll.

Because I knew how much football meant to Grant, I saw my role as being the cheerleader in the background. "You can do it!" I'd encourage him. "You're going to be the best!"

At that time in our lives, I wasn't saying things like, "Oh, we should go home now," meaning that it was time to say good-bye to football and hello to medical school or dental college. The decision to retire from football would have to be his. I clearly remember saying to Grant that if we left football and returned to Dallas, everything would work out just fine.

I took that approach because I knew that if I browbeat him into quitting football, he would resent it for a long time. When the Minnesota Vikings *didn't* cut him loose and paid him to continue rehabbing his knee, Grant hung on to that slender reed. He was still in pro football.

Grant loved the camaraderie of the locker room. Even though he didn't party with his teammates, he enjoyed hanging out with them. He was part of a very small club that tens of thousands of men aspire to join but only a few ever belong to. Although he would never admit it, being part of the NFL was a rush and a huge ego boost for my husband. You couldn't get any higher than the NFL.

I'll admit that my ego was stroked by being part of the "NFL wives" sorority. During the 1986 season, even though Grant remained injured and never suited up, I sat with other team wives—with Sean bouncing on my lap—at all the Vikings home games inside the Metrodome. I developed bonds with the wives and girlfriends as well.

Being married to an NFL player had perks beyond free tickets in the family section. Before the start of the 1986 season, while we were still in Dallas, Grant asked me what I wanted for my upcoming birthday in September.

I thought about how cold it could get in Minneapolis in November and December. I knew what I wanted—a mink coat!

I understand that today wearing a mink coat is one of the most politically incorrect things you can do, but in the late '80s, having a mink coat was a sign of status.

"Do you think I can get a fur coat for my birthday?" I asked one evening while Grant and I dined at a fine restaurant. My parents were babysitting Sean.

Grant thought for a moment. He didn't like making any decisions about anything I wanted to buy. "Sure, sounds good to me," he said.

Mink coats are expensive, but we seemed to have plenty of money in those days. If you want to get a good deal on a fur coat, then shop for one in Dallas in the middle of July. I found a beautiful mink coat at Neiman Marcus for only $1,200 (around $2,600 in today's dollars) that was an absolute bargain.

I checked again with Grant since this was an expensive purchase. This time he said, "Go for it!"

Even though the Vikings played indoors, I enjoyed walking into the Metrodome in my mink coat when the weather turned freezing in November. I bundled up Sean like he was an Eskimo. I'd never been in temperatures so cold, and wearing the mink coat kept me toasty warm. Little did I know that years later, Grant would use my mink coat against me in such a way that I would wish I had never bought it.

And then, just after Thanksgiving, the Vikings coaching staff decided that Grant was no longer in their plans and released him.

Once again, Grant's football days looked to be over. I thought we were going to get serious about medical school or dental college, but within weeks of Grant's release, Seattle Seahawks head coach Chuck Knox said he wanted Grant to play for him. Like many coaches around the league, Knox loved Grant's size and potential. He invited Grant to come to Seattle when the 1986 season was over so that he and his coaching staff could review Grant's rehabilitation status as well as judge his character and temperament in person.

Grant flew to Seattle in early 1987 and was put through a battery of tests—both physical and mental. The coaching staff loved Grant's blue-collar, lunch-pail mentality and work-hard attitude, and they also realized that he was very intelligent and could learn the playbook quickly. The Seahawks needed a backup to veteran center Blair Bush and thought Grant fit the bill. Seattle tendered an offer, which Grant accepted and signed in late February 1987.

Grant came home to Dallas and spent even *more* time in the gym. The knee came around; now the issue was Grant's muscle mass. I remember him saying, "Gee, I just wish I could put some fat on myself," because his metabolism was off the charts. He was still eating a ton of food, but he was losing weight as fast as he was putting it on.

One afternoon in the spring of 1987, Grant came home from the gym carrying a couple of small cardboard boxes.

"What do you have in there?"

"Steroids."

I'd heard of steroids. They were synthetic drugs that increased muscle mass and strength. Grant told me that half the players were "juicing" and that all the defensive linemen used them. I knew what Grant was thinking: *If I want to level the playing field, then I better jump on the steroids bandwagon.*

Now keep in mind that this revelation happened at a time when the NFL did not test players for steroid use. While I had heard of these performance-enhancing drugs, I didn't know that much about their dangers or side effects.

"Where did you get 'em?" I asked.

"From a guy at the gym. They weren't hard to find."

"So you're really going to take them?"

"Yeah, starting right now."

Grant opened both boxes. One contained steroids in a liquid form within vials; the other box held two dozen syringes.

"I need you to shoot me up." Grant grabbed a syringe and jabbed it into a vial to withdraw the steroids.

My eyes must have looked like saucers. "You mean right here?" I asked. We were standing in the living room.

"Yeah. I want you to shoot me in the butt."

"Grant, I've had no training in how to do this. And you know how I hate needles."

"It's not that big a deal. Just stick it in."

With that, Grant walked over to our dining room and leaned on a chair. Then he yanked on his Seahawks shorts and underwear, exposing his butt.

"Anywhere in the cheek," he directed.

"I'm not so sure about this."

"Pretend you're sticking a dart in me. You can do this."

I still wasn't so sure. "Okay. Here goes nothing."

I jabbed the needle, but it was like hitting solid rock. The needle bounced off. I tried two more times with no better results, which frustrated Grant.

"Okay, I'll do it myself."

I handed over the filled syringe to Grant. Then he reached back, stabbed himself, and pressed on the plunger.

What in the world did I just witness?

Thirty years later, I know the answer: I observed a husband who was willing to do anything to be part of the Ultimate Guy Club—the NFL.

CHAPTER 7

ILLEGAL PROCEDURE

I'll say one thing for steroids: they really work.

Grant immediately noticed how his shoulders and back got huge and how much more weight he could lift in the gym. Since his old dress shirts with eighteen-inch necklines were way too tight around the collar, he had to have shirts custom-made with twenty-inch necks as well as custom-tailored pants that fit much better around his waist.

The steroids added bulk to a body that had been going through an eye-popping transformation ever since he arrived on the Abilene Christian campus as a six-foot-five freshman weighing 215 pounds. By the time he graduated from ACU, he had grown two more inches and beefed up his body to 295 pounds, but to play center effectively in the NFL, Grant felt that he needed to be bigger.

A three-month cycle of steroids turned Grant into the Incredible Hulk's twin brother. Grant's weight swelled to 315 pounds, and everyone was in awe of his enormous size. He definitely looked like an NFL offensive lineman.

With muscles on top of muscles, Grant felt like his body was where it needed to be after two seasons on the IR (injured reserve). Head coach Chuck Knox, who probably knew not to ask too many questions, praised Grant's "off-season workout regimen." With a muscleman physique and a repaired knee, Grant was confident that the Seahawks coaching staff would find a roster spot for him during training camp.

And then abrupt news swept through the league with the announcement that the NFL would begin randomly testing players for steroids during the 1987 season.

How did Grant react?

My husband was such a rule follower that he would never consider taking steroids once the NFL outlawed them. He stopped injecting himself right away, but an overriding concern about losing muscle mass and strength motivated him to maintain a strong work ethic in the gym and disciplined eating habits.

Grant felt well prepared for the Seahawks training camp, which was held at the team's training facility on land leased from Northwest University in Kirkland, Washington. Keli McGregor, a tight end trying to make the team, was assigned to be his roommate. This was, as they say, the start of a beautiful friendship. During training camp, however, Keli suffered a wrist injury, which meant surgery and being put on the injured reserve list.

Following the wrist operation, Keli became really, really sick. Grant, being the Good Samaritan, did everything for him—fetching him meals and Gatorade, delivering his mail, and making phone calls for him. What people don't understand is that when football players have surgery during training camp, they go right back to the lonely four walls of a college dorm room. Grant was there when Keli needed a buddy, which cemented their bond of friendship.

Besides looking out for Keli, Grant was a dynamo on the practice field and felt like he was in a good situation. Chuck Knox was as positive a coach as Grant could hope for. "We're going to start Blair Bush at center because of all the experience he has," Knox said during a one-on-one meeting in his office, "but we're grooming you to take his place. We think you're going to be a great center."

Then Knox had a question for Grant. "Have you ever considered deep snapping? Because we're looking for someone to handle those duties."

Deep snapping is a football term for those who hike the ball on extra points, field goals, and punts. The deep snapper, also known as the long snapper, must rocket the football seven or fifteen yards in a perfect spiral to the holder or punter, respectively. Anything short of a 100 percent success rate is catastrophic—and usually results in a lost football game. Deep snapping is a high-pressure job, much like a trapeze artist working without a net. Mess up more than a couple of times, and Grant would be looking at which medical school he wanted to attend.

On the flip side, performing the deep snapping duties made Grant more valuable to the team, which made him less likely to get cut. "Every time I get out on the field, I have a chance to make an impression on the coaches," he said. "It doesn't matter what I'm doing. I have to be the best at what I do."

Naturally, Grant told Coach Knox that he'd love to try the deep snapping. He had long snapped back at Abilene Christian, but Grant hadn't been given that opportunity with the Colts or the Vikings. The Seahawks placeholder on field goals and extra points would be second-string quarterback Jeff Kemp, who was a month older than Grant and also looking to make an impression since 1987 was his first year as a Seahawk.

Jeff, the son of former NFL quarterback and US Congressman Jack Kemp, had backed up Joe Montana of the San Francisco 49ers. He was poised to play behind starter Dave Krieg, who was preparing for his eighth season with the Seahawks.

Jeff had the same nose-to-the-grindstone mentality as Grant. After Coach Knox asked Grant to perform the deep snapping duties, he and Jeff met after practice—after the last wind sprint had been run—and worked on the snap, catch, and set. There were many late afternoons when they devoted a good hour to practicing the snap and hold.

When you spend a lot of hours together, you develop a bond. It turned out that Jeff took his Christian faith seriously as well, and he and his wife, Stacy, became close friends of ours. (When Jeff's eleven-year NFL career was over, he and his family stayed in the Pacific Northwest, where he founded a ministry called Stronger Families. Today, he works with Family Life, a national Christian organization, and has written several faith-building books, including *Facing the Blitz: Three Strategies for Turning Trials into Triumphs*.)

There was another new player on the Seahawks who's worth mentioning—a rookie named Brian Bosworth.

Nicknamed "The Boz" and known for his blond flattop, shoulder-length mullet, and lines shaved on each side of his head, the flamboyant linebacker arrived in Seattle with a lot of media hype. He wanted to wear #44, his old number at Oklahoma, since that had become part of his "brand"; but the NFL prohibited linebackers from wearing jerseys with numbers in the 40s. So Bosworth asked for the next "double" number—#55—which happened to be Grant's jersey number.

One afternoon, the Boz dropped by Grant's locker and asked him if he could have his jersey number. Grant could have told him to go pound sand, but instead he smiled and said, "Sure, no problem." That was so Grant as well. My husband chose a number that would stay with him until the day he retired: #54.

ON STRIKE

What a long road back to the NFL.

After losing two seasons to injury—practically an eternity in pro football—and working as hard as ever to bring his rehabbed body back to the level it needed to be, Grant was on cloud nine when he made the Seahawks' 53-man roster for the 1987 season.

The threat of a player's strike, however, hung over the team and the

NFL like a gloomy fog. For months, the team owners and the National Football League Players Association (NFLPA) had been squabbling over free agency rules that compensated a player's original team with draft picks or players from his new team when the player moved to a different franchise. The players union felt the "Rozelle Rule," as it was called, hampered the ability of players to sign with a new team for more dollars.

Union leadership believed that the players would hold the most leverage if they were to go on strike after the second week of games—having given fans enough time to whet their appetite for a new season. That's exactly what happened.

Locked out from football, Grant and his good buddy Keli McGregor, who was still on injured reserve, hung around the apartment all day, playing with Sean and watching TV. (They didn't sit around drinking beer because there wasn't any alcohol in our home.)

After canceling the slate of games scheduled for the third week of the season, the NFL decided the show must go on. Teams began hiring replacement players. Grant held no grudge toward those athletes, taking the attitude that everything was out of his control anyway. But he felt he had to go on strike because that's what the players union had decided.

Ever the pro, Grant continued to work out at a nearby gym, figuring the strike would be short-lived. There was so much money at stake for the owners, TV networks, and the players, so how long could the strike really last?

After three replacement games, the players union called off the strike and returned to the playing field with nothing to show for their efforts: no changes to free agency rules, no guaranteed share of league revenue, and no collective bargaining agreement.

Grant, a pawn on the chessboard, was just happy to be back in his football routine, and so was I. When the games resumed, everything was soon forgotten as teams fought for a playoff spot and a Super Bowl title. The Seahawks had missed the playoffs the last two seasons and were in a tight race in December when center Blair Bush broke his right hand during the last home game against the Denver Broncos.

I was sitting in the players' family section of the Kingdome when I looked down and saw Grant on the sideline practicing snaps with Seahawks starting quarterback Dave Krieg. Grant was going to play with the first-team offense!

Denver, on the strength of John Elway's arm, had come back from a 14–0 deficit to tie the game. On Grant's *first* snap to Krieg, the exchange was fumbled over to the Broncos. One play later, Elway found a receiver in the end zone, and Seattle was down 21–14.

A fumbled snap is a disaster, and coaches are often quick to blame the center since they have so much invested in the quarterback. Fortunately for Grant, the Seahawks came back to score two touchdowns and win a squeaker, 28–21.

"That malfunction almost spelled disaster," head coach Chuck Knox said after the game; but a win is a win, and it covers a multitude of sins—which allowed Grant to breathe easier. He was ecstatic about the victory and stoked that he was finally playing *his* position—center—in the National Football League. This was everything he had been working for. How he played had *mattered*. Except for the muffed exchange on his first snap, Grant performed well and showed that he belonged on an NFL field.

But bending over and placing one hand on the ball and being part of every offensive play put Grant in harm's way. He got pummeled by behemoth linemen engaged in an all-out war in the trenches. Helmet-to-helmet collisions were commonplace. When Grant remained on the field for punts, field goals, and extra points, an opposing player usually lined up directly across from him. Once Grant snapped the ball, his opponent would smash into him with brute force—but most of the time Grant's head was still tucked between his legs because he focused his eyes on the punter or the holder.

When Grant arrived at our apartment following the Denver game, he had a small plastic baggy in hand that contained several pills.

"What are those for?" I asked.

"Everything hurts," he said. "The team doctor gave me these when I told him I was in pain."

I figured these pills were stronger than the Advil that Grant had been taking for years after practice and games. Advil, an ibuprofen, is an over-the-counter medication used to relieve pain, swelling, and inflammation.

I'm not sure what Grant had in the baggy that day, but they had to be some form of painkillers. Looking back, this was the start of Grant's dependency on addictive painkillers like hydrocodone-based Vicodin and oxycodone-based Percocet, as well as powerful anti-inflammatories like Toradol.

Those after-game baggies became as commonplace as ice packs once Grant took over for Blair Bush. Seattle was in a playoff push and would finish the season with a 9–6 record (the season was shortened by one game because of the strike), but it was good enough to squeeze into a wild card playoff game against the Houston Oilers.

Grant was fired up to be the starting center in an NFL playoff game. I didn't make the trip to Houston because of Sean and the expense (players' wives had to pay their own way), but I was glued to the TV back in Seattle. I felt a bit homesick watching the game because Grant had secured tickets for my parents and sisters in the Seahawks section at the Astrodome. My family made the four-hour drive from Dallas to cheer on Grant.

Late in a close game, a Seahawk player went down at the line of scrimmage, and the head umpire signaled for an injury time-out. I looked to see if the down player was Grant, but then a beer commercial aired. When action resumed, I immediately knew that Grant wasn't in the game any longer. Backup Doug Hire had taken his place. The announcing team didn't mention Grant's absence or talk about why he was no longer playing, so I kept an eye on the offense. When Grant didn't see any more action, that meant only one thing: he had been injured.

The Seahawks lost a heartbreaker, 23–20, in overtime. After the game, I received a phone call from Grant. He was calling from the visitors locker room inside the Astrodome.

"I got hurt," he said.

"Oh no. What—"

"It's my right knee. The team doc doesn't think it's as bad as my left, but I'll need surgery as soon as possible. We're looking at Tuesday afternoon."

This was a blow. As I commiserated with my husband, I could tell that he was greatly upset with his new knee injury. Everything he had worked for to become an NFL starter had slipped through his fingers.

Grant was in a lot of pain when he arrived home. This time he had several baggies in his possession, and he gulped painkillers and anti-inflammatories like they were M&M's.

On Tuesday morning, Keli came over to the apartment to watch sixteen-month-old Sean while I drove Grant to Swedish Hospital in Seattle, where the procedure was done on his knee that afternoon. His medical team kept him overnight in the hospital.

When I brought him back to the apartment, Grant was experiencing significant post-op pain and couldn't get comfortable in our bed. I fixed him up on the couch with his leg propped up so he could get some sleep. That night, the excruciating pain was overtaken by nausea and fever. Grant cried out for help in the early morning hours, and I rushed to his side.

"Cyndy, it's my knee!" he grimaced.

"Let me take a look."

I pulled back his blanket, and what I saw astounded me. His knee had swelled to the size of a basketball! I gingerly touched the skin around his knee. It felt very hot and unnatural.

"I don't like this. I have to call somebody—now!"

"Call Dr. Scranton," Grant said.

Even though it was the middle of the night, I dialed Dr. Pierce Scranton, the team physician, and quickly described the massive swelling.

"This is serious," Dr. Scranton said. "Call an ambulance, and I'll meet you at the hospital."

My heart remained in my throat. I made another phone call and woke up Keli, who agreed to come over and look after Sean while we dealt with this emergency.

Grant was rushed by paramedics to the operating room, where Dr. Scranton drained the knee to reduce the swelling. I maintained a vigil in the waiting room, nervous as a cat. At dawn's first light, I called Grant's parents, whom I knew to be early risers. After describing the events of the last few hours, Pat said, "We'll take the first plane to Seattle."

DeWayne and Pat arrived that afternoon and relieved Keli from babysitting duty. Grant remained very sick and ran a high fever. He was put in a VIP penthouse hospital room, but he was out of it—nearly delirious at times.

Things seemed to be spiraling out of control. I spoke with a grim-faced Dr. Scranton in the hallway, who said Grant had a staph infection in his knee.

"What does that mean?" I asked. I had heard of staph infections but wasn't entirely sure what they were.

"Staph infections are caused by staphylococcus bacteria. Right now, the danger is that the staph infection in Grant's knee is not responding to antibiotics because we can't seem to get the swelling down." Dr. Scranton said he was worried that Grant had been exposed to methicillin-resistant *staphylococcus aureus*, or MRSA, an increasingly common strain of staph bacteria that was being called a "superbug" in medical circles.

"This is a complicated, serious development," Dr. Scranton said.

"How serious?"

"Very serious. If antibiotics don't get this under control, we'll have to amputate his leg."

I was suddenly very afraid.

"I don't mean to alarm you," the doctor continued, "but I want you to be aware of the seriousness of the situation. The next forty-eight hours are key."

Shaken, I thanked Dr. Scranton for his concern and called several players' wives, including Stacy Kemp, asking them to pray for Grant. Then I reached out to our church in Bellevue, and members offered to help any way they could, from watching Sean to setting up a calendar for people to bring over meals.

DeWayne and Pat provided tremendous support during that first week and then returned to their new home in Carlsbad, California, north of San Diego. My parents flew in from Texas so that there would be no gap in "grandparent coverage."

This was a faith-testing time. I was in a daze, and Grant was so sick that he was out of it for days. A port, short for a Port-a-Cath, had been installed beneath the skin near his heart. A catheter connected the port to a vein, which made it far easier for drugs to be administered. In Grant's situation, the port was connected to an IV containing Vancomycin, an antibiotic used to treat bacterial infections like staph. To keep the port clean, it was necessary to hook him up to a bag of saline.

For the next week, I didn't leave his side except when he had to go into the operating room two *more* times to have his swollen knee drained.

"We can't seem to control Grant's staph infection," Dr. Scranton said.

I had seen Grant's knee balloon in size. I had seen the beads of sweat forming on his forehead. I had seen the look of concern in his eyes. Grant knew about the dangers of staph infections and MRSA because of his preparation for medical school exams.

After several more days of prayer and holding my breath, Grant turned a corner when the swelling in his knee noticeably dropped. Vancomycin was working. I thanked the Lord that Grant would not lose his leg. He remained in the hospital for three more weeks as a cautionary measure so that his medical team could keep an eye on the knee and monitor his progress.

The Seahawks organization went the extra mile as well. Our apartment lease expired shortly after Grant's operation, so the team moved us into a beautiful three-bedroom condo on Lake Washington and picked up the tab. The team also paid for a home-care nurse to come by twice a day to check on Grant and administer Vancomycin and cleansing saline. Grant still needed medical care because he was frail and far from 100 percent.

I would say that it wasn't until late March or early April that Grant was back on his feet and looking like his old self. But he was truly never the same after the staph infection. He started leaving our bed in the middle of the night because he couldn't get comfortable. He'd get up and go to the living room, where he'd sit on the couch or an easy chair and watch TV.

I always knew he was gone, and I missed sleeping with my husband.

RUNNING THE OPTION

I remember another part of the conversation Grant and I had when he called me from the Astrodome locker room to tell me that he had injured his right knee.

"So you can't play anymore," I said.

"Not until I get it fixed."

Every time Grant got injured, I thought it meant we were leaving football and going back to Dallas, but Grant saw each injury as just another bump in the road in the life of an NFL football player.

I thought, *I know that your body is your job, but when your body is breaking down, getting injured and hurt, shouldn't you move on to something else? Can't we go on to medical school and be done with football?*

Grant had *many* options at his fingertips. How many professional football players walked around with acceptances to different dental colleges and medical schools in their hip pockets?

Those thoughts never invaded Grant's mind. Not even after nearly losing his leg.

The nursing care stopped in April, but Dr. Scranton didn't take the port out because they wanted to make sure the staph infection remained at bay. That didn't deter Grant from driving himself to the Seahawks team facility to start rehabilitating his knee and getting it mobile again.

Grant wasn't finished with football yet, not by a long shot.

CHAPTER 8

FINDING EQUILIBRIUM

During the spring of 1988, Grant needed two more surgeries to clean out his infected knee joint. The staph infection had done a number on his body, and Grant spent weeks at our Lake Washington condo hooked up to an IV drip of Vancomycin. His medical team informed Grant that he would have to deal with the ramifications of *staphylococcus* for the rest of his life, which meant he needed to practice top-notch personal grooming habits, like washing his hands frequently.

After five years of being married to an NFL football player, it slowly dawned on me that the marriage I envisioned wasn't going to happen. Under those circumstances, we found equilibrium in our relationship: he was the breadwinning professional athlete, and I was the supportive wife. Within these roles, we made the best of the situation we found ourselves in.

I hate to say this, but I really enjoyed the time he was injured. We had time to go out to dinner, see movies, and slowly walk the neighborhood with Sean in tow. We fed the ducks and went on picnics. We had a lot of family time, which was precious to me. I remember thinking, *Gee, this is so normal, living this way. I wish we were like other families and this was our home. I could live like this every day.*

One of the things we loved doing was watching the fishmongers at

Pike Place Market fling white-bellied fish fifteen feet toward the counter and hearing six men yell in unison, "Hal-i-but! Goin' right home!" Strolling through the crowded stalls and shops, rubbing shoulders with flocks of tourists, made for a nice diversion any day of the week.

A block away from the open-air bustle of Pike Place Market was a coffee emporium that everyone was raving about—a place called Starbucks. We both loved their lattes and the coffeehouse vibe.

I remember during one of our coffee dates mentioning to Grant that I was jealous of the people who had nine-to-five jobs. My husband leaned back in his chair and smiled. "People who work nine-to-five don't make the kind of money I make," he said. He had a point, since his salary was pushing $150,000 a year (or $308,000 in today's dollars) as a five-year NFL veteran.

"But I just hate that every year we don't know if you're going to make the team," I said. "Football's so risky."

Grant smiled again. "Well, if you want no risk, then I need to go work at some place like McDonald's." That's not what I wanted for him either, but that spring I made another plea over a Starbucks latte.

"Grant, now that this staph infection has done a number on your knee, please tell me that you're considering not playing anymore. I know you've been sick, and you're doing this antibiotic treatment, but once this is done, can we go home? I don't want anything else happening to you. You've had some major events on your knees, and I don't want you getting hurt anymore." I was tearful and reached for a Starbucks napkin to dry my eyes.

Grant looked at me with his sweet face and angelic smile. He said, without being rude or ugly, "Cyndy, I might as well see what's going to happen because they can't put me on waivers if I'm still injured. Maybe I'll get put on the IR and still make some money. But if I retire, the team is off the hook to pay me anything."

"Yeah, but can you come back and—"

"Starting three games last year showed me that I can play in the

NFL—and then this happened!" he interjected. "I know I can get back to where I was before. Chuck Knox is in my corner because he likes me."

There wasn't much more I could say. There would be no promise of going home, no promise of being done.

I came to a place where I reminded myself to enjoy this time of being semi-normal. I understood that our family life wouldn't be like this once training camp and the season started.

DRAINAGE TIME

After Grant weaned himself from Vancomycin, he started taking an oral antibiotic to keep the bacteria at bay. While rehabbing the knee in the late spring, a small sac of fibrous tissue known as the bursa filled with fluid. His swollen knee looked horrible.

"I have an appointment tomorrow to see Dr. Scranton," Grant said after I expressed concern.

I suddenly had an idea. "Can I join you? I can get a sitter for Sean."

Normally, independent-minded Grant would have insisted that I didn't have to go, but on this occasion, he surprised me. "Sure. I'd appreciate the support."

The following day, Dr. Pierce Scranton, the Seahawks team doctor, didn't like the look of the swollen knee. "We're going to have to drain it," he said. "Sorry, but it's going to hurt like hell."

Grant was stoic and barely reacted. I think he was steeling himself because he knew what the painful procedure entailed. "Do what you have to do, Doc," he said.

Dr. Scranton put on rubber gloves and a mask and went to work. After administering a local anesthetic, my eyes got big when Dr. Scranton reached for a new syringe, which was huge! The gauge of that needle had to be the size of one of my knitting needles!

Grant gripped the examination table as Dr. Scranton worked the syringe under the kneecap. Satisfied that he had found the mother lode, the doctor filled the massive syringe with the nastiest-looking stuff I'd ever seen. Dr. Scranton emptied the green-and-white fluid into a plastic container and returned for more. I'd say he drained a quart or more that day.

I left the doctor's office feeling rather green around the gills. Grant was chipper; he'd just successfully undergone a painful draining of the knee—the first of many, unfortunately, for him. The fluid was tested in the lab and found to contain traces of *staphylococcus*, an indication that the staph infection was still hanging around. For the rest of his career, Grant would receive ice therapy before and after every practice and game. Bags of chipped ice were wrapped onto his right knee (and often his left knee as well) to stem the swelling. "Ice is nice," he would say, but ice therapy still didn't negate the necessity of having his right knee drained periodically.

Despite the uncertainty of whether his right knee would come around, despite the hassle of getting his knees iced every day, and despite the presence of *staphylococcus* in his bloodstream, Grant wasn't going to walk away from the NFL until he was pushed out the door. The only thing he could control was the amount of effort he put into preparing his body for the rigors of pro football, which was what he set his formidable mind on.

There was another aspect fueling Grant's bullheaded desire to make a comeback. Now that he had experienced what it was like to be the *starting* center—to hear his name reverberating throughout a full stadium when the offense was introduced during pregame ceremonies, to feel the electric energy of a game-winning drive with fans on their feet screaming for a victory—Grant didn't want to step away from the NFL. He had become a bona fide warrior, forging unbreakable bonds on the field and in the locker room.

This was his reward for persevering through five seasons, for putting his body through incredible punishment on the practice field and in NFL stadiums—including two years of rehabbing from a knee injury. Three games as an NFL starter gave him a taste of what it was like to have a supporting role in the most popular sport in America, which was played before millions of people watching the games on television.

In Grant's mind, everything he was doing to prepare himself to play professional football was for the good of our family. That's how he provided for us, from a roof over our heads to food on the table to some of the nicer things in life—travel, jewelry, a mink coat—and a home back in Texas. Granted, the house in Rowlett sat empty for a year and a half while Grant was rehabbing in Seattle, but we were building equity.

Grant, ever the goal setter, came up with a fresh set for the start of the 1988 Seahawks training camp, which he kept in his Bible. They went like this:

- Cyndy and Sean are all that Matter
- Finance your Education
- Sean will be Proud of my Effort
- Cyndy and Sean Will Always Love Me

Grant didn't have any rhyme or reason why he capitalized certain words, but looking back in time, I'm surprised Grant included "Finance your Education" on his list. I think Grant still *hoped* he would go to medical school or dental college someday, or maybe he added that goal because he knew how much I wanted him to leave football and start a career in medicine. But he rarely talked about becoming a doctor or dentist anymore. His mind was focused on the Holy Grail of professional sport—the National Football League.

There was a different edge to Grant as he started the 1988 season. It didn't matter what I thought or wanted; he was going to play football.

Looking back, his thought process was starting to change. He wasn't being logical after nearly losing his leg to a football injury.

BACK IN THE SADDLE

Grant wasn't 100 percent during training camp, but the Seahawks coaching staff believed Grant was on the mend and could still perform the deep snapping duties. Grant's spot on the team was safe for another season.

When I got the good news, I asked him, "Since you're making this much money, can we talk about having another child?"

I had just turned twenty-nine years old and could feel my biological clock ticking. If we were going to have four children, we needed to get going. I loved being a mom, which fulfilled me in many ways. Sean had turned three, and I didn't want him to be too old to play with a brother or sister.

When I explained all that to Grant, he didn't say anything, but I could see the wheels turning in his head. "If you go off birth control now and get pregnant as quickly as you did last time, then the baby would arrive in the off-season," he said. In his football-centric mind, this would work for him. "Okay, we can try."

Now keep in mind that our love life wasn't all that . . . regular . . . but we made it work. My heart's desire was to have another child to love and someone else to love me. Once again, I got pregnant quickly.

The morning sickness seemed more bearable this time around. I had girlfriends from our church—I was attending the Bellevue Church of Christ, where I found a great faith community—who'd come over and pick up Sean during the first trimester when I wasn't feeling that great and needed to lie down on the couch.

One time during the middle of the season, I asked Grant, "Hey, can you take Sean to school for me in the morning?" I was dragging and feeling poorly.

Grant shook his head. "I want to be at the complex at 7:00 a.m., so I can't be late," he said. "I work. You'll have to take Sean to school or find a carpool for him."

Grant wasn't trying to blow me off or be mean, but I do remember thinking, *Gee, I thought marriage is where people help each other*. Our roles were clearly defined: I was the homemaker who did the laundry, prepared and cooked our meals, kept the apartment picked up and clean, and saw that Sean was well cared for. Grant brought home the bacon by playing football. His office was the 53-yard-by-100-yard football field.

Although he didn't have to punch a time clock when he arrived at the Seahawk training facility, in Grant's mind, he was "late for work" if he wasn't inside the locker room by 7:00 a.m. or shortly thereafter. (Depending on the day of the week, the players were generally expected to report sometime between 8:00 a.m. and 9:00 a.m. for team meetings, weight training, and practice.) Grant used the extra time to get treatment for nagging injuries and prepare his body for the next game. He also got taped before every practice and liked to have certain trainers wrap his wrists, hands, ankles, and feet because they taped him the way he wanted to be taped. Grant didn't want to wait in line for a specific trainer he liked.

Grant worked himself back into football shape and had a solid year with the Seahawks during the 1988 season. He even got to start a couple of games when Blair Bush went down with an ankle injury. The Seahawks won their division with a 9–7 record and returned to the playoffs for the second straight year, but they lost in the first round to the Cincinnati Bengals.

What I remember most about that season is that Grant would always take Sean to the team facility on Tuesdays, his supposed day off. Sean, four at the time, would have the run of the locker room while Grant was iced, massaged, and tended to for lingering aches and pains. I appreciated the chance to rest while Sean tagged along with Dad at the Seahawks headquarters. I knew that Sean absolutely loved the attention he received from these gargantuan men.

Back in our apartment, Sean had a pop-up tent in his bedroom because he thought he was an "outdoors man." At bedtime, Grant would squeeze his big body into Sean's tent and read a Dr. Seuss book. These were special father-and-son times.

An ultrasound at sixteen weeks revealed that we were going to have a girl, which was exciting news for both of us. When we found out, Grant said to me, "That's great news, but I don't know much about girls." I understood. Grant hadn't been around young children as much as I had growing up. He had a sister, but she was older, and Grant had never been a babysitter or taught Sunday school classes like I had. But he was definitely excited about having a daughter. "We're getting a girl and a boy in two tries," he said. "That's awesome."

Sarah Elizabeth Feasel was born May 20, 1989. Sarah was an easy baby who had a way of pacifying herself. We were both grateful Sarah didn't have fits or cry a lot. She nearly fit into the palms of Grant's oversize hands, prompting this second-time dad to say, "She's a little angel."

A FREE AGENT MOVE

Three months before Sarah's birth, in early February 1989, the Seahawks had to declare twenty members of its fifty-seven-man roster as free agents in an effort to offset an antitrust lawsuit brought by the NFL Players Association after their twenty-four-day strike in 1987. One of the players left unprotected was center Blair Bush, a twelve-year veteran who was thought to be too old to be attractive to other teams. Grant, who had a lot of upside, was one of the players protected by the Seahawks.

The Green Bay Packers, however, swooped in and snatched up Blair, creating a huge opportunity for Grant to take his colleague's place on the line of scrimmage. When Grant heard the news that Blair was no longer a Seahawk, my husband quickly developed the eye of the tiger. In Grant's mind, the center position was his for the taking.

Once again, Grant devoted gobs of time to the gym, working on fortifying his knees and building up his strength. As he worked on getting in tip-top shape, his attitude was this: *I'm going to get up early in the morning, I'm going to get it done in the weight room, and I'm going to stay as late as necessary to rehab my knee and get my body into the right shape.*

When he kissed us good-bye and left for training camp in July, we both knew the center position was Grant's job to lose. Except that Grant couldn't run any longer; his knees protested too much. He used to jog to stay in shape, but that sort of exertion stopped after the staph infection. Instead, Grant concentrated on being big and strong. He used to say, "I'm not the strongest guy on the team and am definitely not the fastest guy, but I am big and I am strong."

Even though Grant usually came in last on running drills, Chuck Knox still loved the way he controlled his area on the line of scrimmage. When training camp broke, Coach Knox named him as his starter, telling an Associated Press reporter, "We've won with Grant Feasel at center before, and we think we can win with him now."

Playing every offensive down was a lot harder on Grant's body. Every game, his knuckles were torn up and bruised from the hand-to-hand fighting that happens on the line of scrimmage. Even today, when I look at action shots of Grant, I see how his uniform was stained by blood from cuts on his knuckles. I worried about the abrasions and bruises because of his staph infection.

When he was off the field, he regularly popped anti-inflammatory medications like Advil in his mouth, reaching into his Levi's jeans pocket that was always filled with the oxide-red pills. After games, he always brought home a baggy containing several doses of the prescription painkiller Vicodin.

Once a starter, Grant began receiving "numbing injections" before the game—a local anesthetic named Marcaine that would mask pain at least for the next three or four hours. The use of painkiller shots only minutes before the opening kickoff was pervasive in pro football, Grant said. "Everyone does them," he said. "If it wasn't for these shots, a lot of players wouldn't be able to suit up."

From then on at every home game, I had this mental picture of Grant submitting his backside to a syringe filled with a painkiller, a practice that was legal in the NFL. Teams were required to keep records of all the prescription medications administered to the players, as well as the post-game baggies of Vicodin, which wasn't comforting at all. Grant wasn't that fazed by it. He saw the pregame shots as a necessary evil. Now that he was a starter, he was going to do what it took to stay in the lineup and not let his teammates down.

Not letting his teammates down . . .

There was a play during Grant's first season as a starter that haunted him until the day he died. What happened during a field goal attempt, in which Grant was the deep snapper, became part of an NFL Films blooper reel and ESPN SportsCenter's Not Top Ten Plays of the Week—goofy background music and all.

It all started during a tight October game against the Denver Broncos when the Seahawks field goal unit lined up for a thirty-five-yard try. Grant leaned over and wrapped both hands around the football, readying himself to deliver a speedy snap to his holder and good friend, backup quarterback Jeff Kemp. Waiting to deliver the kick was Norm Johnson, who was in the midst of an eighteen-year kicking career and known for his reliability. This was the third season that this triumvirate had worked together.

Jeff got down on one knee and looked over the Denver defense. He saw several Broncos stacking the left side of the line. Jeff cupped his hands and yelled, "Watch it, left!"

Grant thought he heard Jeff yell, "Red set," which was the signal to snap the ball without hesitation. When Grant rifled the ball between his legs, Jeff's head was turned toward his kicker. The fast-moving leather football nearly stuck in the earhole of Jeff's helmet before bouncing away. There was a scrum for the ball, which Jeff recovered, but it didn't matter since the Broncos received the ball on downs anyway.

Rusty Tillman, the Seahawks special teams coach, was known as a "freaker" on the sidelines because of the way he would yell, scream, and generally freak out when something went wrong on special teams. This was one of those occasions, and he got in Grant's face and unloaded on him. I don't know what was said, but the miscue turned out to be a costly one because the Seahawks lost in overtime by a field goal, 24–21.

Grant had a long face when he exited the Seahawks locker room at the Kingdome. He was a perfectionist. He wouldn't even purposefully make bad snaps in practice when Jeff Kemp asked if he could have a few low or high snaps to prepare himself for an errant hike. For Grant to have one of his snapped balls turn into a disaster that lost the game devastated him.

We didn't say much on the drive home. That night, he took his Vicodin and sat in his easy chair with his remote, bouncing from channel to channel to listen to what the local sportscasters and football pundits on ESPN were saying about the botched snap. I believe he was traumatized by what happened that Sunday afternoon. He kept saying, "I'm never going to get over this."

He was right. Fifteen, twenty years later, when Grant would get drunk in our bedroom while watching a football game, all it took was watching another center muff a snap and Grant would say, "Yeah, but I had the worst snap of all time."

The day after the debacle in Seattle, Grant didn't want to go to the team facility because he had so much anxiety. He was worried that Rusty Tillman wasn't done yelling at him, but he also feared what Chuck Knox would say during the team meeting in front of the other players.

When Grant came home that night, I asked him, "Well, was it as bad as you thought it was going to be?"

"You tell me," he replied.

"So what did Chuck say?"

"He said, 'When I'm in my last days and confined to a nursing home and connected to an iron lung at the end of my life, my last thoughts on this earth will be, *Why in the heck did Grant Feasel snap that ball into Jeff Kemp's head in our game against Denver?*'"

The footage got replayed so much on ESPN and in the blooper films that Grant received some notoriety. Bruce Nash, the author of several books that highlighted strange and embarrassing moments in football, interviewed Grant for his book *Football Hall of Shame 2,* released in 1990.

"When I went home after the season, that play was the only thing my friends wanted to talk about," Grant told Nash. "They thought it was hilarious, but it wasn't funny to me. But I won't be snapping the ball into Kemp's earhole again without making damn sure that's where it's supposed to go."

The Seahawks fell short of the NFL playoffs with a 7–9 record. Aside from the botched snap, the 1989 season was a success for Grant, who started all sixteen games and acquitted himself well.

What happened against Denver chastened Grant, however. You'd think that after he'd become a starter that he could relax a bit and smell the roses, but Grant lived in fear that he was one more bad snap away from the unemployment line. He had a mantra going:

You're only as good as your last game.

The herd keeps moving.

They will flush you down the toilet like a dead goldfish.

After one season in the starting lineup, Grant's desire was to ride the NFL wave as long as he could.

Little did we both know that a wipeout was in our future.

CHAPTER 9

THREE AND OUT

The 1989 season was the beginning of a three-year stretch in which Grant would start forty-seven consecutive games in the NFL. This happened when he was between the ages of twenty-nine and thirty-one, a period when he relied more on his experience and "street smarts" in the trenches than on his diminishing athletic skills.

It was all part of a grand bargain that he made with himself: *I want nothing more than to play in the NFL, so if I wreck my body in the process, then that's the price I'm willing to pay.*

This was the prevailing attitude among NFL players back then, and—I'm sad to say—it's what I hear countless pro football players still saying today. Grant did play one more season in 1992, but he was limited to deep-snapping duties as he backed up starting center Joe Tofflemire. And then Grant was done.

The herd keeps moving.

These were also the three years when Grant fulfilled his dream: a starting position on an NFL team that paid him his greatest salary—$625,000 annually (or $1.1 million in today's dollars).

Grant had to earn his spot on the offensive line after Blair Bush left for greener pastures in Green Bay because the Seahawks invested a second-round draft pick in Joe Tofflemire, a first-team All-American center out of the University of Arizona, during the 1989 NFL Draft. The "Fighting Feasel" beat out Joe at training camp each summer, but that's just as much because Joe had his own set of nagging injuries to deal with—back and shoulder problems. Joe had suffered a shoulder injury while at Arizona that would require nine surgeries during his playing days, as well as a shoulder replacement after he retired from the NFL. Four screws were implanted to keep his spine in place.

Joe was a six-foot-three-inch massive presence just like Grant. He, too, died an early death on September 27, 2011—nine months before Grant passed away—that shook my husband nearly as much as Keli McGregor's sudden demise. Joe Tofflemire died of heart failure at the age of forty-six, an unforeseen death that "devastated his family and jarred friends who struggled to reconcile such a thing with the sculpted athlete they once knew," wrote John Blanchette in the *Spokane Spokesman-Review* newspaper.

They will flush you down the toilet like a dead goldfish.

Any thoughts about what Grant was doing to his body while starting *fifty* consecutive NFL games at center—if I include the last three games of the 1988 season—were swept under the artificial turf inside the Kingdome. He did what was necessary to get ready for the next game, from dipping into his pocket for more Advil every couple of hours to faithfully taking Vicodin painkillers from Sunday night to Monday night. Grant made sure he got his body worked on before and after practice, including ice therapy on his knees.

I'll tell you something about Grant that reveals a great deal about his character: He didn't seem to be much different when he was a starter than when he didn't play. That's how incredibly dedicated Grant was to football and as an employee of the Seattle Seahawks. He always wanted to be the best he could be.

I'm grateful that our son, Sean, witnessed Grant's commitment to excellence at an impressionable age. Sean was in his early elementary school years when his father was a three-year starter, old enough to begin noticing Grant's can-do attitude. (Sean shares his father's tenacious work ethic today.)

As a six- and seven-year-old boy, Sean took every opportunity to hang around the locker room or practice field, where other players—who also looked like giants to our towheaded son—would come over to Sean and say things like, "I know you're proud of your dad," or "Your dad was great today," or "Your dad may have a lot of pain, but he still keeps going. Your dad's a good guy."

Sean heard and received these things that were said about his father, but our son was also smart. He knew that Dad left the apartment early and didn't come back until late. He knew that Dad came home with ice packs wrapped in cellophane on one or both knees, and he knew that Dad had limitations on some of the things he could and couldn't do. Grant could toss a football back and forth with Sean, but he couldn't chase after his pint-size son who wanted to "run" with the football. Grant could stand and shoot a basketball at a hoop, but he couldn't guard a first-grader in a little one-on-one contest in the driveway. And Grant wasn't even thirty-two years old.

Despite the toll on his body, these were really good years for us. I'm not talking about the money. I'm talking about Grant being happy. He was more at peace during this period than most of the time we were married because he was seeing the fruit of what he was working for. His application for membership in the Ultimate Guy Club had been accepted. His place in the locker room was secure. Grant felt that he'd made the right decision to continue playing in the NFL and not go back to medical school. He exuded an air of self-satisfaction that he'd done the right thing.

During this special time when Grant started all these games, I never said, "I'm sick of this football life. I hate this. I want to stop this. I see what it's doing to you." There was never any of that.

I adapted. I always took his cue. When he was happy and came home happy, life was good. Sure, Grant stepped through the apartment front door with an ice bag strapped to his right knee and Band-Aids on his knuckles, but he was glad to see the kids and acted happy to see me. We loved the times we had together, and I must say that he was an attentive dad to the kids when he was home in the evening. Because the kids always came first, which is the way we wanted it to be. He liked reading bedtime stories to Sean and Sarah and maybe watching a kids' movie on TV with them. There were times when he would lie in his easy chair with the ice bag on one knee and a compression sleeve on the other knee, and they would climb on him.

There were a lot of heavy sighs from Grant, however. Things hurt. The kids saw the "ow-ees"—the cuts on his hands and forearms and the purplish bruises on his forehead and neck. They sensed his limited mobility and were respectful. Despite Grant's inability to get on the floor and roughhouse with Sean and Sarah, my children have memories of their father being very attentive to them.

Grant wasn't as attentive to my needs. He was too tired to be engaged most of the time; there was only so much gas left in the tank. "Date nights" were few and far between during the season. He didn't enjoy going out because he was fatigued. He usually wasn't recognized at restaurants—remember, offensive linemen are practically anonymous—but when he was greeted by fans, Grant was unfailingly polite and engaged, which depleted more of his energy stores.

The biggest minus was our love life. This was a time when I had an active boy in elementary school and a verbal preschooler, so I was a busy mom. My life was running back and forth to school and doing errands and taking care of the kids—feeding, dressing, and bathing duties. At the end of a long day, I valued—and needed—cuddle time.

One night, when the kids were down and we were watching a little TV, I said to Grant, "Gee, we don't ever have sex that much anymore."

"Well, we can on Tuesday nights."

Tuesday was Grant's day off, although he still went into the team facility for treatment anyway. This was his way of saying that he was too tired to perform on any other night of the week. Tuesday night would have to do.

So I said yes to the arrangement. That made our love life a bit mechanical and not very spontaneous, but once again, I went with the flow. Tuesday nights it would be.

I was an NFL wife, remember?

SPINNING THEIR WHEELS

After reaching the NFL playoffs in 1987 and 1988, the Seahawks of 1989 and the early '90s were an average team. During Grant's starting tenure they failed to qualify for the NFL playoffs.

No matter the team's record, watching your husband play professional football is a nerve-racking experience. The saying *You're only one play away from never stepping on the field again* was always in the back of my mind, but it was still neat to be part of the NFL experience because Grant played so much. He participated in *every* offensive play since he also snapped the ball on all punts, field goal attempts, and points after touchdowns.

After every home game, the players' families had passes to wait in a secured room between the Seahawks locker room and the visitors locker space. That was enjoyable, too, talking with other wives and girlfriends and meeting family members. Sean was "special" because he got to steal away and enter the Seahawks locker room, where he played among the discarded jerseys and shoulder pads with other kids. As for me, I sometimes caught glimpses of famous players like Howie Long of the Raiders or John Elway of the Broncos walking the hallway, usually trailed by camera crews hungry for a sound bite. That was fun too.

It would be a good ninety minutes before I saw Grant. It took time for the trainers to unravel yards of tape around his hands, knees, and ankles, apply dressings to scraped knuckles and elbows, and massage the kinks in his back.

After his shower, beat reporters from the *Seattle Times*, *Seattle Post-Intelligencer*, and regional newspapers dropped by his locker for a quote. The media doesn't usually interview centers, but Grant was so cooperative and always had something interesting to say that the local sports people made him their go-to guy after the game. Grant never refused an interview, even during the practice week.

Grant was known as a stand-up football player and a stand-up Christian guy. Everyone knew that he was going to be at the team chapel on Sunday mornings, and coaches and teammates were aware that Grant took his Christian faith seriously. Throughout my husband's NFL career, we were part of a couples' Bible study that met on Wednesday nights in one of the player's homes. If there was a Bible study at the training facility, Grant was there.

When the local Fellowship of Christian Athletes chapter would ask him to speak to a high school football team—say around seven o'clock, when his practice day was over—he would say yes to those early evening engagements. But since he was always one of the last to leave the Seahawk training facility, he paced himself with those speaking requests. Grant only did a handful during the season, and the major reason was because he wanted to get home to see the kids before they went to bed.

Grant also participated in community events, such as visiting cancer wards at local hospitals or handing out presents to sick kids at Seattle's Children's Hospital. It was all part of being an NFL player and another reason why Grant was so content during his starting years.

A NEW POST-GAME RITUAL

No matter how well Grant played—and he didn't have many poor games—and no matter if the Seahawks won or lost, he made sure he tuned in to the local news as well as ESPN to watch game highlights. He wanted to judge himself before going in to watch film on Monday. He also liked me to watch the highlights with him, and he used me as a foil to share thoughts on how and why a certain play worked or got blown up. I watched so much football with Grant over the years that I knew every guy he played against by name and the head coach of every NFL team.

Once Grant won the starting position at center, he took his job so seriously that he seemed to be in a continual state of high anxiety. He wanted to be the best he could be.

One time—this would have been a few games into the 1989 season, when Grant became a starter—he put the kids to bed after a Sunday game. Instead of flipping on the TV to watch highlights, he grabbed a coat and his car keys and headed toward the front door of our apartment.

"Going somewhere?" I asked.

"I'll be right back," he replied. "I'm going to the 7-Eleven to pick up some things." The convenience store was just a couple of blocks away.

"The fridge is full. I even have your favorite ice cream . . ."

"I'll be right back," he said with a smile as he left the apartment.

When Grant returned, he was carrying a brown bag.

"What did you get?" I was curious what prompted this Sunday night trip to 7-Eleven.

"A little something to help me relax."

I followed Grant into the kitchen, where he took out a six-pack of Coors Light—in twelve-ounce longneck bottles—from the brown paper bag. He opened a cabinet door and grabbed one of the many plastic cups he'd collected from area restaurants. A church key flipped off the cap of the first bottle. Grant tipped the bottle of Coors Light into a plastic cup, careful not to pour too fast. Drinking out of a cup was new: back in our college days, he always drank straight from the bottle.

Grant didn't offer me a beer that night. He knew I hated the taste. Diet Cokes and Starbucks lattes were my guilty pleasures.

I couldn't figure out what was happening. The whole scene was weird. First of all, why didn't we stop at the 7-Eleven on the way home from the game to save Grant a trip? As for the drinking part, that was out of character because I'd never seen Grant have a beer *in* season. Sure, he sometimes sipped on a Coors Light or some other brand at a summer party or back in Texas during the off-season, but he was a Boy Scout once he went to training camp.

Like I said before, we never had any alcohol in our Seattle apartment, so watching Grant drain a Coors Light in his easy chair while clicking through TV channels was unusual.

When Grant finished his cup, he returned to the fridge and opened another bottle of Coors Light. When he was done, he went back . . . and back . . . and back . . . until he drank the entire six-pack in one sitting.

I sat on the couch, flipping through the Sunday paper, in utter amazement. One, two, three, four, five, six beers . . . went down the hatch and rather quickly. Sure, they were only twelve-ounce servings, but something told me it would be better not to ask him what the heck he was doing. When he finished number six, Grant raised himself slowly out of his chair and set the last empty bottle in the Coors Light six-pack carrier. Then he placed everything into the brown paper bag and walked to the front door.

"Where are you going?" I asked.

"To the trash."

"Oh."

When Grant returned, he said he was tired and went straight to bed—and slept like a log. I know because I heard the snoring.

I was still processing what happened the following day. Grant wasn't tipsy after drinking all that beer, but his mood was . . . *tranquil.* That

Monday, Grant repeated the same sequence of events: waiting until the kids were in bed before making a quick run to the 7-Eleven to buy a six-pack of Coors Light. He downed all six and then tossed the empties into the trash.

Now this was getting *really* weird. I knew that it wasn't normal behavior to bring a six-pack of beer into the house, drink it all in one sitting, and then make sure the empty bottles were no longer in the apartment.

"What's with the beer?" I asked. I used my inquisitive voice, not an accusatory tone.

"It's just something to take the edge off."

"Isn't that what the Vicodin is for?" Grant had brought home another baggy with a handful of the popular painkiller.

"Oh, Cyndy." Grant made a face. "Now that I'm playing so much . . ." Grant's voice trailed off.

I wouldn't let it go. This hiding behavior wasn't him. This wasn't the Grant I knew.

"This isn't your deal," he explained. "This is my deal. You take care of the kids, you take care of yourself, and I'll take care of myself. Don't worry about me. I'm in a lot of pain, and I'm just trying to manage it."

Starting with the 1989 season, Grant's way of managing his postgame pain became the Sunday night/Monday night beer-and-Vicodin cocktail, if you will. As for why he was going to great lengths to be secretive about his 7-Eleven beer hauls, Grant explained that he didn't want Sean to see him bringing home a six-pack of Coors Light. My husband knew that Sean was smart, impressionable, and bright enough to figure out that Dad was having a beer.

Later, Grant would concentrate on hiding his drinking from me.

CHAPTER 10

LOST YARDAGE

The story of Grant's final season of professional football really started the year before in the summer of 1991, when Grant was still the starting center, still at the top of his career.

During four seasons in the Pacific Northwest, we had developed a familiar rhythm. At the end of training camp in late August, I arrived in Seattle with the kids and UPS delivered boxes of clothes and knickknacks to our apartment in Redmond, which was near the Seahawks training facility in Kirkland. Our condo apartment was decorated with nice rental furniture, and we even leased a TV. Renting stuff made things a lot easier when the season was over. All I had to do was organize the return of the furniture and electronics and hand the keys back to the office manager.

Sometime in late August 1991, I flew into Seattle with our two children. Sean was about to turn six years old, and Sarah was a little over two years old. This time around, we rented a player's house in Bellevue so that the kids could play outside. Jeff Chadwick, a Seahawks wide receiver who got traded to the Los Angeles Rams, owned the home.

Since I was a few weeks away from celebrating my thirty-second birthday, the thought occurred to me that if Grant and I were going to have four children—like we talked about before we got married—then I needed to take a more proactive approach, even though I had stopped taking birth control pills after Sarah's arrival. (I really didn't like how awful the Pill made me feel.) So we took other precautions, meaning we paid attention to my monthly cycle.

After reuniting with Grant after training camp, I brought up the topic of having another child. Since conceiving a baby during the football season meant an off-season delivery, he was fine with trying. As long as Tuesday nights worked for me.

Hey, I took what I could get, especially when I thought the timing was right. Wouldn't you know it: Once again, I became pregnant right away. And once again, I felt sick and threw up more times than I could count. Nausea was my constant companion. No surprise there.

Sometime in mid-November, I went to my ob-gyn for a second ultrasound. I was probably twelve weeks along in my first trimester.

A nurse technician applied gel to the transducer and rubbed my abdomen while looking at the monitor. A frown crossed her face. She made several more passes and then stopped.

"I'm not finding a heartbeat," she said.

My world stopped. "What do you—"

"I'm going to get the doctor," she replied. "I'll be right back."

Suddenly, my mind traveled in a thousand different directions. The first ultrasound had been routine, and a heartbeat had been detected. And now this.

Dr. White (not his real name), who'd been the obstetrician for several Seahawk babies, quickly entered the ultrasound room. He traced the transducer across my stomach while keeping his eyes locked on the monitor. Then he let out a loud exhale.

"Cyndy, there's just not a heartbeat. I'm sorry."

Tears welled in my eyes. I was too stunned to say anything. Slowly, reality sunk in. My baby was gone.

"Why? What happened?" I managed to say.

Dr. White placed a hand on my shoulder. "Sometimes the body takes care of a pregnancy that's not going to be viable in this manner. I have no other explanation."

I stifled a sob and was close to losing control.

Dr. White leaned closer. "I know you're upset. Let's get in touch with Grant. I know you would like him to be here."

"He can't leave practice." I knew I couldn't call the Seahawk training facility and ask them to hunt down Grant and tell him what happened. That wasn't an option.

My doctor understood. "Tell you what," he said. "Talk to Grant when he gets home tonight. Tell him everything. In the meantime, I'll have the nurse schedule a D&C first thing in the morning."

In those pre-cell phone days, Grant didn't know anything had happened until he stepped through the front door of our apartment. I rushed into his arms and dissolved into tears.

"The baby . . . they couldn't find a heartbeat." My voice was shaking. "I had a—"

I buried my head in his chest. I couldn't bring myself to say the right word. So Grant filled in the blank.

"You mean a miscarriage?"

I nodded, and Grant immediately became downcast.

"Cyndy, I'm just so sorry, but everything will be okay."

I told him about the D&C procedure that I was scheduled for in the morning. "Can you go with me?" I asked.

Grant stepped back. "I can't come because it's during practice."

He didn't have to give me a reason. As an NFL wife, I didn't have to ask why. The following morning was a Thursday, one of the most important practice days of the week, as Grant always told me. Then again, I had never known a day when football practice *wasn't* important.

Grant wrapped his massive arms around my shoulders as I choked on tears. "That's okay. I'll find someone to go with me," I said. Once again, I was trying to be the good soldier.

RECEIVING SUPPORT

The following morning, before 8:00 a.m., Grant was long gone for the Seahawks practice facility. With Sarah in a car seat, I drove Sean to school and then came back home. The babysitter arrived to look after Sarah, and then Connie Millard, wife of Seahawks right guard Bryan Millard, came to the house to give me a ride to the hospital. Bryan, thirty years old and six months younger than Grant, lined up next to Grant on the offensive line and was in the final season of his career.

Connie drove me to the Swedish Medical Center, but I wasn't a good conversationalist. My mind was contemplating what lay ahead: the dilation and curettage (D&C) procedure that would remove tissue from inside the womb. Walking into the hospital without Grant, getting checked into pre-op, and then going under general anesthesia contributed to an out-of-body experience. When I woke up, I was aware that it was over and that Grant wasn't in the waiting room. That made me feel incredibly alone and unsupported.

Following recovery, Connie drove me back to our rental home. I was in a daze, and I barely remember anything about that moment. I did appreciate Connie's support at such a sorrowful time.

The only bright spot was that Grant's parents had arrived and were looking after the kids. The previous evening, we had called DeWayne and Pat as well as my own parents to deliver the bad news about the miscarriage and how I was having a D&C procedure in the morning. Grant's parents said they'd drop everything and take the first flight they could book. They were closer and more available than my parents.

DeWayne and Pat, who had saved the day on previous occasions, were great. When Grant got home sometime after 7:00 p.m., he was caring and attentive, but I was barely hanging on. I felt out of it, especially because I was taking medications to even out my hormones or whatever they did to make the bleeding stop. I will confess that I had a mental set-back at that point and was mentally in a fog.

Normally, I'm an up, happy, *yeah, we-can-do-this* type of person, but everything had been upended by the miscarriage. I cried a lot. I grieved because I had lost a baby. I couldn't stop sobbing or acting emotional. Given my raw reaction, I couldn't imagine ever feeling *normal* again. Looking back, I was probably dealing with depression.

Seeing me this way freaked Grant out. He didn't know what to do with me. "What can I do to help make things better?" he asked after din-ner one evening several days later.

"Nothing," I replied. "Nothing at all."

My greatest wish was to get my old life back. For several weeks, while going through the motions of caring for our two kids, I became distant and strange. I can't explain why I acted this way since I didn't have a strong attachment to the baby—I wasn't that far along. That didn't diminish the deep sadness I felt, however. An unborn child had died—our baby.

When Grant was available, he tried to help, but he was too ill-equipped to know what to do. How could he know? *I* didn't even know how to get back to feeling like my old self. This was a volatile time in our relationship, and my melancholy continued throughout the rest of the 1991 season.

Grant played well, starting all sixteen games and handling the deep snapping duties without a hitch, but the Seahawks finished 7–9 and fourth in the AFC West division. After three seasons of missing the play-offs, head coach Chuck Knox and the Seahawks agreed to part ways at the end of the 1991 season, which is a nice way of saying that Chuck resigned before he was fired. Chuck had a good run in Seattle, coaching for nine years and taking the team to the playoffs four times, but in the NFL, coaches are on a short leash.

The days of "Ground Chuck"—the media's nickname for Chuck Knox because of the way he preferred grinding out yards on the ground rather than through the air—were over. Chuck's style of smashmouth football impacted Grant's health because more running plays meant that my husband got tangled up on the line of scrimmage more often—and took more blows to the head.

That "three yards and a cloud of dust" football philosophy changed when Tom Flores, a former quarterback for the pass-happy Oakland Raiders, became the new head coach. Grant was a known entity to Coach Flores because he had been the Seahawks general manager for the last three seasons. He, too, liked Grant's leadership in the locker room and on the field, but in training camp, Grant lost his starting job to Joe Tofflemire.

I think Tom Flores and the Seahawks coaches decided to give Joe a shot after he rehabbed from shoulder injuries because they believed it was Joe's time. Grant told me he was never really able to compete for his job and that he pretty much expected things to shake out that way.

Nothing changed with Grant's deep snapping duties, however. Ever since my husband zinged a football into the earhole of Jeff Kemp's helmet, he hadn't messed up one deep snapping opportunity on points after touchdowns, punts, or kicks. In fact, Grant had gone three seasons without a miscue, which is why he still had a job.

As a deep snapping specialist, Grant had a high-pressure occupation. Even though he was on the field for only a handful of plays, he could still count on taking a big hit every time he snapped the ball to the holder or punter. Grant was used to that, however, and always wanted to be in the middle of the action, to be contributing to the team.

Besides standing on the sidelines while the offense was on the field, there was the frustration of losing a lot of games. The Seahawks finished 2–14—tied for the NFL's worst record with the New England Patriots—which didn't make football very fun during the 1992 season.

One Tuesday night, on his off day, Grant asked me to get a sitter so we could go out for a bite to eat. This would have been around Thanksgiving time with a month to go in the 1992 season. We didn't go out that often, so I squealed with delight.

As the main course was taken away and we waited for our desserts to arrive, Grant cleared his throat. "I've been thinking about what it would take for me to play football next year," he began.

I shot Grant a quizzical look. "What do you mean?"

"Look, I can deep snap for a few more years and make a lot of money doing that," he said, "but I think I'm done when this season is over."

I nearly spewed a mouthful of water but tried not to show how excited I was. Grant had said before that the NFL would have to carry him off the field, that he would never quit playing football until he was no longer physically able to answer the call.

And now he was saying that he was going to quit before he got carted off the field—or before Coach Flores wanted to see him in his office with his playbook.

I met Grant's eyes. He was serious about retiring. He didn't look like a defeated man, but he was resigned to the fact that his days of playing professional football were rapidly racing toward the finish line. The Seahawks were going to have to find someone else to perform the deep snapping duties when he walked away.

I think this was Grant's rationale: *I'm nearing the end of my career, and I don't want to drag Cyndy and our two kids up to Seattle one more year. Being part of an NFL football team and what this meant to my body isn't worth the pain anymore. I need to be done.*

"Are you thinking about medical school?" I wondered aloud. That thought was always in the back of my mind.

"I don't have to make any decisions at the moment. Let's just get home and we'll figure out what to do from there."

I didn't ask Grant to change his mind or beg him to keep playing, even though if he'd said he wanted to deep snap for a few more years I wouldn't have protested. The money was too good. We both knew that whatever Grant's next job was, he wasn't going to earn anything close to the handsome paychecks he received every two weeks during the season. Remember, Grant was knocking down more than $600,000 a year, which is like a million-dollar salary today.

"That's fine, Grant," I said. "I'm 100 percent behind you, no matter what you do."

Shortly thereafter, Grant asked for a meeting with Coach Flores and informed him that he was retiring when the season was over. As expected, Tom wished Grant all the best and told him he understood.

The last time Grant put on an NFL uniform was on Sunday, December 27, 1992, for a home game against the San Diego Chargers. What a bittersweet day. Grant soaked in every moment, telling himself that this would be the final time he would be taped up, put on a Seahawks uniform, jog onto the field after the first-team introductions, and fulfill his deep snapping duties.

When the final seconds ticked off a 31–17 defeat—and the end of a dismal season—I watched Grant linger and take his time circling the perimeter of the football field. We were sitting in our usual section inside the Kingdome, but this time I had brought along both children: Sean, seven at the time, and Sarah, three years old. I thought it was important for them to witness Dad's final game as an NFL player. Grant took his time in the locker room, no doubt going to every player and coach and thanking them for their part in making his NFL dream a reality. He cleaned out his locker and kept his scuffed-up helmet as a souvenir.

When we greeted Grant in the family waiting area after the game, I saw relief etched on his face. There was no celebratory dinner at a fine-dining establishment like Seattle's Metropolitan Grill that night. Instead, we drove to the Red Roof Inn near the Seattle-Tacoma International Airport, where we would spend the night and take a nonstop flight in the morning to Dallas-Fort Worth. Grant was ready to get home. He didn't want to stick around Seattle any longer and be reminded that he was no longer in the NFL.

We were all ready to go. I had packed up our belongings, arranged for UPS to pick up the boxes, and handed the keys back to one of Jeff Chadwick's friends.

I can't remember where we grabbed a bite to eat, but what leaves an indelible memory in my mind is what happened later that evening. I had just finished putting the kids to bed in an adjoining room (with the door open between the two rooms), when I looked over at Grant, sitting on a garish couch. In his left hand was a large plastic cup half-full of a dark-colored carbonated drink, which I figured was Diet Coke—his favorite drink as well as mine.

Then I spotted a bottle down at Grant's feet—a bottle of Jack Daniel's, the famous down-home malt whiskey from Tennessee.

For the second time that season, my jaw dropped. I had *never* seen Grant consume a drink made with hard spirits. When I saw him reach down, grab the glass bottle, and pour a healthy shot of Jack Daniel's, I really didn't know what to say. But I did think, *What in the world are you doing?*

I decided on the spur of the moment to play it cool, just like I had when he brought home a six-pack of Coors Light on Sunday and Monday nights, got blitzed, and carried a half-dozen empty bottles to the trash. My husband had just played his final game of football, so maybe he was commemorating the moment in a special way.

As for how he got the Jack Daniel's, I don't know when or where he purchased the bottle of hard liquor, but I was well aware that whiskey packed a bigger wallop than beer.

"Grant, you need to slow down," I said. "We have to get on the plane tomorrow."

"Don't worry about me." Grant grinned and took another long swig. "I'll be okay. I'm just relaxing and doing a little celebrating. My NFL career is over. Let's open those presents we got ourselves."

Grant stood up and found two small gift-wrapped boxes in his carry-on luggage.

"Here," he said, presenting me with one of the boxes. The other one was for him. I knew exactly what was inside.

After Grant had told Coach Flores about his plans to retire, my husband took me shopping for a new watch. Actually, I didn't need a watch. I had a stainless steel Rolex that worked just fine, and Grant had an identical Rolex as well. But as a way to commemorate the end of his NFL career, Grant suggested that we buy his-and-hers *gold* Rolex watches.

I opened up my present, flushed with excitement. Grant did the same. When we ripped open the wrapping paper, there they were: matching gold Rolexes that cost—if my memory is correct—$5,000 each. Actually, mine cost more because my Rolex came with tiny diamonds around the dial.

I admired the way the gold Rolex looked on my left wrist. When I leaned over and kissed Grant to thank him, the smell of alcohol was on his lips.

I pulled away. The smell of alcohol bothered me. If Grant noticed, he acted like nothing happened. "Cyndy, I got something else for you," he said.

I looked at Grant, whose eyes were glassy like marbles. He was having trouble focusing.

"What? You already gave me something. I love my new Rolex—"

Grant reached into his carry-on bag and took out another gift-wrapped box—the type of box that a young man presents when he is about to propose.

"I want to give you an early anniversary present before we get on the plane tomorrow. We have a big one coming up—our tenth."

Grant was right. Our tenth wedding anniversary was twelve days away, on January 8, 1993.

"How thoughtful of you." I accepted a beautifully wrapped white box with a small red ribbon and wondered what was inside.

I quickly opened the box. Sitting atop a velvet pad was an eighteen-karat gold band with diamonds all around.

I sucked in my breath. The ring was stunning—but Grant had given me the exact same ring three years earlier for our seventh anniversary! In fact, I was wearing that ring right next to my wedding band.

"This ring is beautiful . . . but I've got one just like it already." I showed Grant my left hand. Next to my wedding ring was a gold band sprinkled with diamonds, just like the ring he had just presented me with.

Grant suddenly sobered up, but his face was confused. I held up the new ring next to the one on my ring finger. "See? You've already given me a ring identical to this," I said.

"I did?"

"Yeah, Grant."

I couldn't believe what was happening. He didn't remember that he had given me a gold-and-diamond band exactly like the one in the velvet-lined box and I was wearing it on my ring finger.

What an awkward moment for both of us. Then I had an idea. I slipped on the new gold band with diamonds next to my wedding ring and the other gold band with diamonds. I had to admit that the triple layer of stunning jewelry was impressive.

I thanked Grant with a warm kiss. He meant well. He had just forgotten, that's all.

I was tired and went to bed. Grant, however, stayed in his chair, sipping his whiskey and Diet Coke, alone in his thoughts. I remember falling asleep with an unsettling feeling in the pit of my stomach.

The old Grant would have been way too sharp to do something like that.

CHAPTER 11

THE POST-NFL SEASON

When Grant retired from the NFL, he was thirty-two years old. Neither he nor I knew that he had twenty years to live.

Those two decades can be summarized in two sentences: One, within months of retiring, Grant never went a day without drinking alcohol and became addicted to prescription painkillers. And two, we were both clueless about how the collisions and concussions from playing football had addled his mind to a point where our marriage would be ruined, our family destroyed, and Grant would die as a direct result of his excessive drinking.

The average football fan has no idea of the punishment that's dished out every time the center snaps the ball. Helmet-to-helmet collisions happened all the time when Grant played, and those types of collisions continue today. Helmets are supposed to prevent players from receiving a skull fracture or a broken neck, but the way the game has developed over the years, the players use their hard-plastic helmets as battering rams and powerful weapons to hit each other even harder. While no one wants to go back to the old "leatherhead" days, modern helmets give football players a false sense of security. There's no helmet in the world that can protect players from concussions or completely buffer a blow.

In Grant's case, the heavy head-to-head hits rattled his brain and wrenched his neck. When a fast-but-sturdy nose guard rammed him or "the pile" fell on top of him, Grant's body took a wallop as well. Muscles were bruised, and ligaments and joints were stretched and sometimes torn.

Keep in mind that Grant played much of his career on unforgiving artificial surfaces that were like patio carpet rolled onto a concrete slab. The first generation of artificial turf wasn't very sophisticated and lacked the "give" of a traditional dirt-and-grass field or today's softer FieldTurf, which is found in many big stadiums. Since Grant played half his games on the rock-hard artificial surfaces laid down inside the Kingdome, as well as in stadiums like the Astrodome in Houston, Three Rivers in Pittsburgh, and Riverfront in Cincinnati, he suffered a lot more wear-and-tear on his body.

The violent collisions that sent Grant tumbling to the ground were all about timing and leverage. My husband knew about Newton's second law of motion—that force equals mass times acceleration—which is why he spent so much time preparing his body for Game Day. Mass was his weight, which is why Grant was so focused on gaining bulk when he started playing in the NFL. Acceleration was how quickly Grant could get onto the balls of his feet and deliver a heavy physical blow to a behemoth nose tackle or blitzing linebacker coming at him.

Each impact lasted one- or two-tenths of a second, which doesn't sound like a long time, but when you're an integral part of an offense that runs sixty-six plays per game (the average number of offensive plays for an NFL team), those body-to-body crashes add up, especially when you get hit two or three times on the same play.

Grant often complained of "stingers" on Sunday nights. A stinger was an injury to a nerve in the upper arm, either at the neck or shoulder. A stinging or burning pain spread from his neck to one of his hands and felt like an electric shock down the arm. Many times I heard him say, "My neck is on fire."

Grant also said this phrase after a lot of games: "I got my bell rung today." What he meant was that he got knocked on the head so hard—usually from a player's helmet or knee—that he saw stars or heard ringing noises inside his skull. Grant tried to shrug off those aftershocks. Saying he got his "bell rung" was a football way of diminishing the significance of a concussion.

Knowing what I know today, I wish one of us had paid more attention when he said his awareness of his surroundings was altered on the field, which meant he might have suffered a concussion. Since a brain scan or an X-ray can't detect concussions, Grant had no idea how many violent shocks his brain experienced from the days of playing pee wee football to his final game in the NFL. Football players like Grant didn't like to acknowledge to their coaches that they had been "dinged," since that could result in being taken out of the game. The warrior mentality that permeated the football world meant that they had to suck it up to keep playing.

Concussions weren't well understood during Grant's era and were viewed by players as something on par with a sprained ankle. Coaches didn't think a concussion meant that the injured player was done for the day. They relied on a trainer to ask a few perfunctory questions—"How many fingers am I holding up?"—and then wave a broken capsule of smelling salts under the player's nose so that he could get back into the game and help the team.

Grant played through many severe blows to his head, but one concussion stands out in my memory because Grant explained it in great detail to me, which was highly unusual. One Sunday night, Grant came home from a road game at Mile High Stadium, where the Seahawks had taken on the Denver Broncos. While watching the game on TV back in Seattle, I noticed that Grant missed a couple of offensive series.

"How come you went out of the game?" I asked as we settled on the couch to watch Chris Berman and ESPN SportsCenter.

"I was snapping an extra point when I got my bell rung," he said.

Centers weren't protected from getting hit after snapping the ball on punts, kicks, or extra points when Grant was in the NFL.

"Everything went black," he continued. "I saw nothing but total darkness. Then the sound of the deafening crowd hit me. I couldn't see a thing, so I wasn't sure how I could get to the sidelines. I stumbled around until someone helped me off. The entire time, my head felt like it was going to explode, especially because the crowd noise was earsplitting. It was excruciatingly loud at Mile High."

"But you went back in."

"I did. Don't ask me what happened out there because I don't remember a whole lot. My head still hurts like crazy."

Years later, when Grant was drunk in his easy chair, he would shake his head and tell me, "You have no idea what I'm dealing with or what kind of pain I'm in."

I know now that it was because he'd gotten his bell rung so many times.

A NEW ADDITION

When our family of four flew from Seattle to Dallas after Grant's last game, I was excited that our off-season home—which we had purchased in 1989 when it was being built in Rockwall—would become our permanent residence. Rockwall was six miles east of Rowlett and only twenty minutes or so from my parents' home in Garland.

Our four-bedroom, three-bath home at 1410 Meandering Way was really nice and spacious with 3,389 square feet. Even with a bright open floor plan, decorative crown molding, and vaulted ceilings, the price was well within our means. I think we paid around $175,000 for a home with a brick facade and lots of curb appeal. For the money that Grant had made in the NFL, our home was very affordable.

The location was great too. We lived in a country club neighborhood known as The Shores that was ideal for young families—quiet and safe—with a community pool where the kids could swim. We were also an easy fifteen-minute drive from Dallas Christian School, my alma mater, in nearby Mesquite, where Sean was a third grader and Sarah was old enough for Dallas Christian's preschool program.

Excitement was in the air. It felt good to establish roots in the community and be near my family. I was thrilled that Grant wouldn't be leaving me and the kids for training camp when July rolled around. Since he had his whole life in front of him—a blank canvas—I wondered, *What's he going to do?*

A month or so after we arrived in Rockwall, we got a sitter and went out for dinner to our favorite Texas BBQ place. We were talking about our future, so I took the opportunity to ask him if he was still interested in going to medical school. "We'll find a way to get it done with two kids, and my mom would love to help out," I said. "We can still do this, you know."

Grant cut me off with the wave of a hand. "I'm too old. Why would I want to become a dentist or a doctor now? It'll take years and cost us a lot of money to make that happen."

"But you have to do something," I said. I knew the money we had saved up wouldn't last forever, and I had no idea what his investments were or how they were doing.

"There's no rush on getting a job," he said. "I have the rest of my life to work."

"But can we afford—"

"We're doing fine. Everything's under control," he said.

Grant had always handled our family finances, keeping the bills and credit cards paid and balancing the checkbook. I had a single credit card and a checkbook but no ledger to track how much money was coming in or going out. That's the way Grant wanted to do things. Consequently, I never knew how much money was in the checking account or how much money we really had.

What did Grant do during his first few months of retirement from pro football? Since there was no urgency about finding a new career, he drove the kids to Dallas Christian in the morning and then went to a nearby gym, where he worked out. That's what he'd been doing every off-season for the last ten years, so he felt comfortable with the routine. He liked maintaining the well-developed muscles on his body, although he complained that his metabolism was slowing down and that he was putting on weight. He wasn't vain, but he knew that people looked at him because he was so big and tall, so he wanted to look like he was in great shape.

Grant kept himself busy by building a deck in the backyard with one of his gym buddies and buying a Labrador, which we named Buster, for the kids. My husband also played more golf, a noncontact sport that his compromised body could enjoy, although neck and back pain kept him from playing more. He had to ride in a cart since he couldn't walk eighteen holes. Grant, being athletic, could hit the ball a mile. The golf ball didn't always travel straight, but he played well enough to be known as a respectable golfer. He liked playing in charity golf tournaments where he was one of the "celebrities," which was an ego booster.

As we settled into our post-NFL lives, I must say that Grant was attentive to the kids and me—as if to make up for all those years when football consumed him. He was more relaxed and always up to playing board games with the kids. He read books to the kids at bedtime, as long as they weren't anything longer than *If You Give a Mouse a Cookie* or a chapter in *Goosebumps*. What he loved most was taking Sean and Sarah to family movies like *The Lion King* and *Toy Story*.

He also showed spiritual leadership by taking us to church on Sunday mornings. It felt good being part of Saturn Road Church of Christ, the congregation I had grown up in and where we were married more than a decade earlier. We made friends with couples who had young children and enjoyed an active social life.

Better yet, Grant and I resumed the practice of a weekly date night, which brought us closer together romantically. Back in the early days of our marriage, I thought physical intimacy was an important part of our relationship. We had great sex, but it was never regular and tapered off during the last half of Grant's NFL career. Once we were back in Rockwall, we rekindled our love life, which was important to both of us but especially to me.

You see, I could still feel a hole in my heart from the miscarriage and wanted another child. A year and a half later, I was prone to periods of feeling glum and not my perky self. I liked being a mom and felt that was my calling, so I never did go back on birth control pills. Trying to have another child was fine with Grant, but it wasn't happening as quickly as it had before.

In June 1993, six months after Grant's retirement, we took a family vacation to the West Coast and visited Grant's parents in Carlsbad. They had a time-share that they let us use at Tamarack Beach Resort across the street from the Pacific Ocean. We loved going to the beach, where Sean learned to boogie board and Sarah played in the sand. Our favorite restaurants were Harbor Fish Café, which had great fish and chips, and Cessy's, a hole-in-the-wall taco shop that we loved.

Maybe it was the beauty of a Pacific sunset or the relaxation one feels at a beachy vacation spot, but I conceived a child during the trip. I was overjoyed when a home pregnancy test delivered the good news, and Grant was happy for us as well. We didn't tell family or friends for weeks, though, because I wanted to be overly cautious since my last pregnancy ended in a miscarriage.

While Grant was genuinely excited by the news, I could also tell he needed time to process what a third child would mean to our family. Left unsaid was whether this child would make it to full term.

I had another rough start and was more nauseated than usual. I needed to have a home health nurse administer an IV several times. Grant did his part by being extra helpful with the kids. Even though I was miserable during the first trimester, I really wanted this child—a child who would complete our family. And then I would get my tubes tied since my pregnancies had been so difficult.

UNFINISHED BUSINESS

Life was good in Rockwall, especially because Grant was developing a special father-son relationship with Sean.

Grant bought dirt bikes—off-road motorcycles designed for rough terrain—for Sean and himself, and my husband loved taking his son out riding in the backcountry. Sean was just eight years old at the time, but he learned to handle a small dirt bike quickly and loved the speed and thrill of catching air. Grant had grown up dirt biking in the Mojave Desert, so sharing this exciting recreational activity with his son was special. They enjoyed dirt biking so much that they went to motocross events, where they watched the professionals soar over massive jumps and kick up mud in the corners. Grant also taught Sean to fire a shotgun and fish for bass.

Although Grant's focus was on Sean, he also paid attention to Sarah, who was just starting school. He was a good father to both kids.

Now that he was out of football, Grant wanted to take care of unfinished business: his crooked nose. Grant's nose had been broken several times during his NFL career and was slightly tilted. His not-so-straight nose didn't bother me, but I wasn't looking at myself in the mirror like he was every morning. He also complained of sinus problems.

When he told me that he wanted to get his nose fixed, I told him to go for it. Grant sought out a plastic surgeon and underwent a rhinoplasty procedure. The nose-straightening operation was a success, and Grant came home from the outpatient surgical center with a prescription for Vicodin, the same painkiller he took on Sunday nights and Mondays when he was playing in the NFL.

I didn't think anything of it at the time. Of course Grant would be taking Vicodin following surgery to straighten his nose. Vicodin was a popular painkiller, but I was unaware that this prescription medication contained an opiate called hydrocodone that causes feelings of euphoria by altering the way the brain perceives pain.

"Hey, can you get me a refill?" Grant asked a couple of weeks after his surgery.

I was the one who went to the drugstore to pick up prescriptions. "Do you really need a refill?" I asked. "What if you don't need them?"

I had grown up in a family where we didn't keep unused prescription medicine around the house. Once the injury was healed or the disease was over, we tossed leftover pills in the trash. We respected the power of these medicines.

"I'd just like to have them in case I need them," Grant said. "And see if you can get one more refill out of this prescription."

I wish his request had raised a red flag with me. Little did I know that starting with his nose surgery, Grant would always have a supply of prescription painkillers like Valium or Percocet on hand until the day he died. He needed something stronger than Advil, which Grant popped like breath mints from a supply he kept in his front pocket.

But Grant was doing something else to take the edge off—something I didn't catch on to during his first eighteen months of retirement. Every evening that we were home, Grant and I fell into a routine after we put the kids down. Grant would head to the kitchen, where a leftover Styrofoam cup from Sonic Drive-In was on the kitchen counter. I think Grant was Sonic's best customer, at least when it came to ordering Diet Cokes. Once a day, sometimes twice, he stopped at a nearby drive-thru to pick up another "Route 44" of Diet Coke. When he got home, he'd refill his Sonic cup with cans of Diet Coke stowed in a second refrigerator inside our garage.

That's why I didn't think it was any big deal when I saw Grant walk into the garage after the kids were in bed. He was reaching for two Diet Cokes, flipping open the pop tabs, and pouring the low-calorie soft drinks into his oversize Sonic cup.

Afterward Grant would retreat to our master bedroom, where he plunked himself down in a soft easy chair and reached for the remote. He loved watching action movies or catching up on the world of sports on ESPN.

I, on the other hand, loved winding down with a good book or a cross-stitch or needlepoint project from the comfort of our family room couch. Sometimes I had the TV on in the background with CNN, local news, or a show like *Twin Peaks*, which was filmed in the Seattle area. (We visited the set one time.) I was a voracious reader of the latest bestsellers, romance novels, self-help books, biographies, and even cookbooks. I was a hyper person—and still am—and found that reading calmed me down.

By 10:00 p.m., I was ready for bed. Grant would be in his easy chair, usually in the middle of a movie. His taste in TV was different from mine: he liked watching sitcoms like *Seinfeld* or MTV for their music specials, as well as action films.

When I was sleepy, I'd walk in our bedroom and say, "Hey, can we turn the TV off?"

Sometimes he'd click off the program or the film, but on other occasions he'd ask if he could finish what he was watching. I would say that was fine and would try to fall asleep as best I could.

There's something else I wish I had paid more attention to—the empty Sonic cup on his nightstand. At the time, though, all I thought was, *Wow, if I was drinking that much Diet Coke, I'd never be able to sleep.*

Looking back, this was the start of a dysfunctional marriage relationship—the drifting apart. Instead of spending the last couple of hours of the day together, we were carving out separate lives. Grant and I used to love watching date night movies together, but as we entertained ourselves in separate rooms, the chasm between us widened.

CHAPTER 12

CHALLENGE FLAG

After getting through the first trimester of my pregnancy, I relaxed a bit. My frame of mind was helped by the knowledge that for the first time in probably twenty-five years, Grant wasn't putting on pads and a helmet after Labor Day weekend. There was life after football after all.

Each ultrasound appointment, however, was like undergoing a stress test, but I got through them. We learned that we would be having another boy. Until he was safely in my arms, I was deeply worried about him. It wasn't until I reached my eighth month of pregnancy in early 1994 that I finally breathed a sigh of relief.

Toward the end of March, my water broke. Grant rushed me to the hospital, where I was prepared for delivery. Everything was advancing well until my ob-gyn realized that the umbilical cord was wrapped around the baby's neck while he was still in the birth canal.

"He's turning blue!" my doctor yelled out, barking orders to the nurses. The atmosphere in the birthing room suddenly changed. I looked at Grant, who was dressed in hospital scrubs. He squeezed my hand and said everything was going to be all right.

The next thing I knew, my doctor shoved the baby back into the womb. "We're doing a C-section," he announced, and that's the last thing I remember.

When I woke up, I was in a recovery room, attached to an IV drip and monitors. I looked around and was terrified.

Grant approached the side of my hospital bed.

"Where's the baby?" I asked. Panic rose in my chest.

Grant took my hand. "We have a big boy. There were a few complications, but he's going to be okay."

"Thank you, God!" I exclaimed. I closed my eyes and whispered a heartfelt thanks to the Lord. When the doctor came into the recovery room, he explained that since our son's Apgar score (used to gauge a newborn's health) was lower than he liked, he was whisked to the neonatal unit, where he was attached to monitors and put on oxygen. "But everything's looking good now," my doctor said. "He's going to be fine. You can see him soon."

When Spencer David Gregory Feasel was placed in my arms, a sense of calm and peace overwhelmed me. Born on March 21, 1994, Spencer was the biggest boy in the nursery at eight pounds and thirteen ounces. Since we were doing S names with our children, we chose the name Spencer because I loved the name. As an added bonus, he was born on DeWayne Feasel's birthday.

My C-section necessitated a two-day stay at the hospital before I was discharged. You'd think after bringing three children into the world that I'd be an old pro with a newborn, but on our first night home, our baby boy cried a great deal, which stressed me out. Fortunately, my mother was there to assist me, and we took turns soothing the little guy. Grant was AWOL. I figured he was in our bedroom, watching TV while Spencer was giving his lungs a workout. I carried Spencer to the bassinet in the master bedroom, where I found Grant fast asleep in his easy chair. The TV blared in the background. On the nightstand next to his bed was a tall Sonic cup.

I had no idea that Grant was drunk on the night we brought Spencer home from the hospital.

FINDING WORK

I hoped that having a third child would awaken Grant to the reality of finding a job. He had gone more than a year without gainful employment or a paycheck, but since I had no idea of how much money we had, I was in the dark. I didn't know how worried I should be, which created anxiety in and of itself.

Even though I was married to Grant and deserved to know the state of our family finances, my husband regarded me as the mother of his children and the parent who kept the home fires burning. He would handle the money. He didn't help me in the kitchen or the laundry room—those were my jobs. But he got the mail every day and took the trash out. I would later learn how significant these two chores were.

Spencer was a few months old when Grant came home from working out and told me about a guy he'd met at the gym who was in medical equipment sales. This fellow said his company had a position available in the Dallas-Fort Worth area, and Grant said he was thinking of applying for it. Since my husband hadn't shown any inclination to look for any sort of job, I naturally encouraged him to check it out. Perhaps a career in medical equipment sales would be right up Grant's alley, given his interest in the field of medicine.

Grant agreed with me. "What's it going to hurt?" he asked. "I might like being a sales rep for a medical company."

This postpartum, hormonally challenged mom felt relieved. The company was called Hill-Rom, one of the biggest makers of hospital beds, hospital furniture, and other health care equipment. Grant was put through a series of interviews, which went well. When the human resource managers learned he played in the NFL, that's all they wanted to talk about, so Grant told engaging stories of lining up against defensive linemen such as Reggie White and Bruce Smith or dealing with play-busting linebackers like Lawrence Taylor and Jack Lambert.

When Grant got the position, he told me that he had been hired to sell "capital equipment" to hospitals. The reality: Grant was a hospital bed salesman, which I thought was way beneath his intelligence—a long way from dental or medical school.

My husband didn't mind, however. "I didn't get to go to medical school, but this position is still in the medical industry. The field is highly interesting to me."

One of the fringe benefits of becoming a sales rep for Hill-Rom was that Grant could work from home. His territory was the Dallas-Fort Worth Metroplex plus large parts of Texas. Most of the time, he drove to health care firms, large and small hospitals, and medical care companies in and around Dallas, which meant he was usually home by six o'clock.

At this point in our marriage with a growing family, I was happy that Grant had *any* sort of job.

AN INADVERTENT DISCOVERY

Not long after Grant was hired by Hill-Rom, I was putting clean laundry away in a walk-in closet that we shared.

My hand touched something between a stack of collared shirts and his underwear. I felt a . . . velvet bag. I immediately knew what was inside the purple pouch: a large flask of Crown Royal. This was a big bottle, a 1.75-liter container.

When Grant got home that night from work, I told him about my discovery. "What's a bottle of whiskey doing in the closet?" I asked.

Grant adopted a nonchalant attitude. "Oh, that? I won it at a golf tournament."

"Then why was the whiskey hidden under your clothes?"

"Because I don't want the kids to find it."

"The bottle was open and half-empty."

"Well, sometimes I pour a little into my cup at night. It helps me to relax."

That sounded weird to me. "Really? Whiskey helps you relax?"

"Some nights I have trouble falling asleep because I'm in so much pain."

"What kind of pain?" I asked.

"Well, my neck hurts. My back bothers me. And my knees hurt."

"So you're drinking because you have all these aches and pains."

Grant nodded. "You got it."

While I was sympathetic to the discomfort Grant felt, hiding a bottle of whiskey and pouring some into his Diet Cokes every night upset me. Apart from when he'd gotten drunk at the Red Roof Inn on the day he retired from the NFL, I had been unaware that he was mixing whiskey with his Diet Cokes before he went to bed every evening.

A lightbulb went off in my head: Grant was drinking to self-medicate. I suddenly understood why Grant preferred to disappear into our bedroom each night, carrying a Sonic cup filled with Diet Coke. Behind closed doors, he'd top off his oversize cup with Crown Royal. He had to be pouring a lot of "fingers" of whiskey because he was often asleep when I came in.

I felt deceived by his behavior. The reason I hadn't put the pieces together until now was because my husband didn't have hangovers. He would awaken in the morning fresh as a daisy, take the kids to school, and go about his day. Yet Grant's secretive manner threw me for an emotional loop because he violated a trust between us. I stuffed my feelings down and didn't confront Grant as I should have, which was the start of a codependent relationship that enabled Grant's growing addiction to alcohol to gain even more traction.

After having my world rocked—and noticing alcohol on Grant's breath now that I knew he was drinking regularly—I wondered what else he was hiding. Call it a woman's intuition.

We had two sinks in the master bath and kept our toiletries in separate cabinet drawers and medicine cabinets. I decided to open his drawer one day when he had left to make some sales calls. Among his lotions, cologne, and shaving blades were two brown bottles with prescription labels for the same painkilling medication—Percocet.

One bottle was nearly empty, and the other was full. I looked at the date the prescriptions were filled. They were a couple of weeks old—very recent. It had been more than a year since he had his nose fixed, so that could mean only one thing: Grant was regularly taking painkillers to go along with his drinking.

The revelation shocked me. I never would have dreamed that Grant would be taking pain medication, which was scary to me. I had heard that it's never a good idea to mix alcohol with pain medications, yet that was exactly what Grant was doing.

I recognized the doctor's name on the label. I remembered that Grant had made an appointment to see him when he complained about his knees. Grant always wore a sleeve on his worst knee—his right—and didn't have the greatest mobility. His knees hurt a lot whenever we had a cold snap, and he had a lot of arthritis. Grant already knew that he was a strong candidate for a double knee replacement, but he didn't want to go under the knife just yet. Grant, thirty-five at the time, felt he was too young to consider the operation. Since replacement knees had a track record of lasting only twenty years, he wanted to wait, figuring this was a once-in-a-lifetime deal.

I accepted Grant's explanation, but he *could* have had a knee replaced and undergone a second replacement later in life, although doctors say the second knee replacement can be less successful. Either way, there was another reason why Grant didn't want a knee replacement or to undergo back or neck surgery to relieve his pain: he was afraid of getting a staph infection. He brought up that reason time and time again.

Finding the pair of bottles filled with a prescription painkiller raised a red flag as well as a question: Had Grant become a drug addict from taking Vicodin after every game?

For the rest of our lives together, Grant was always figuring out how he could get his hands on more prescription painkillers. He found that his best chances were when he found a friendly doctor who'd listen to him describe why his neck was bothering him or his bad knees aching like crazy or his back feeling stiff and sore.

I'm sure he was hurting. He'd always say to me, "I can barely turn my head," and I believed him every time I watched him drive and switch lanes; his neck barely swiveled. Watching him contort his massive body to get into a car—even our Suburban—was a reminder that nothing was made for his size—from SUVs to rental cars to golf carts to seats in the cinema. His height and his size were a blessing on the football field but a curse in everyday life.

When Grant saw an orthopedic specialist or a family physician, he had an agenda: leave that office with a prescription for a painkiller. It wasn't that hard. All Grant had to say was, "Doc, I really got messed up in the NFL. My neck is really bothering me, and my knees are killing me," and he would get a prescription. What other option did modern medicine have?

Self-medicating with prescription painkillers . . . drinking Crown and Diet Coke every night . . . Grant didn't know it, but he was dragging our entire family into darkness—and making decisions that would ruin our family.

A BIG MOVE

One of the best parts about living in Rockwall was being near my family. My parents and two sisters and their families were a fifteen-minute drive from our house, so we saw each other fairly often. "Cousin time" was great, too, because our kids loved playing with their relatives. Attending Saturn Road Church of Christ with my extended family made us even more close-knit.

Grant, of course, didn't have any family in Texas, but DeWayne and Pat usually came out for Christmas and stayed with us two or three times a year. Grant's sister, Linda, lived in Long Beach, California, and Greg lived in Denver, so we rarely saw them.

Most holidays and long weekends were spent with my family. One time we drove to Red River, New Mexico, where my brother-in-law's family owned a wonderful cabin in the mountains near Taos. We made the long driving trip so the kids could play in the snow and learn to ski at the Red River Ski Area.

One afternoon, we gathered in the cabin's living room to play dominoes while keeping an eye on the kids and their snowball fights.

"Where's Grant?" one of my sisters asked. He'd been gone for a good hour or so.

I went into our bedroom, where I found him lying on the bed with a Styrofoam cup in his hand and the TV on.

"Are you kidding me?" I said. I knew exactly what Grant was doing: drinking. Grant knew that no one in my family drank alcohol, which is why he must have brought a private stash with him.

"I'm not bothering anybody. I'm just lying here watching TV."

"Yeah, well everybody else is out in the family room playing dominoes."

"So?"

I told my family that Grant had a headache and had to lie down. They'd heard that excuse before, but Grant didn't care what my family thought. He didn't act that way when we visited his parents in Carlsbad, but when we took family vacations to Gulf Shores in Alabama or Destin, Florida, Grant carried water bottles filled with vodka. When he thought nobody was looking, he'd pour some of his "water" into his Diet Coke. Very tricky, but our kids caught on to this when they were older.

When Spencer was a toddler, we were invited to my parents' home for Thanksgiving dinner. "I'm taking the Pathfinder," Grant announced. "You can take the kids in the Suburban."

"What? We're not going together? Why two cars?" I asked.

"So I can leave when I want to."

That was a horrible idea—and I told him so. This was Thanksgiving, a time when families gathered together to celebrate an important holiday. I said it would be rude if he left before everyone else, but Grant didn't care. His mind was made up.

"Sorry, but that's what we're doing," he said. There would be no further discussion.

That night, after the pumpkin pie had been served, Grant made some excuse about his neck bothering him, and he was gone. I'll admit that I saw some raised eyebrows around my parents' dinner table. I felt extremely embarrassed.

The two-car scenario would happen for the rest of our marriage whenever we were invited over to a family member's home in the Dallas area. As soon as Grant thought he could skip out, he excused himself, saying he was tired or his neck hurt.

Why was Grant in such a hurry to make a getaway? Because he wanted to get home and make up for lost time with his Crown and Cokes.

One evening in early 1996, Grant came home from a business trip to Indiana. He gave me a light peck on the cheek and placed his briefcase on the kitchen counter.

"I've been doing some thinking, and I think we should move closer to the airport," he said.

That sounded like a terrible idea. "Why do you want to do that? It's only an hour from Rockwall to DFW. How much closer do you have to be?"

"Yeah, but I'm going to be doing all this flying. It'll be a lot easier for me to get to DFW if we live further west. I won't get stuck in traffic like I do now."

I didn't get it. He didn't fly that often for business. He only flew occasionally to Texas' major cities—Houston, Austin, and San Antonio—and traveled by air to Hill-Rom's headquarters in Batesville, Indiana, for corporate sales meetings or to meet reps from various hospitals and health care companies who wanted to see the factory. But that was only once a month or so.

Most of the time, Grant was having breakfast or lunch meetings in and around Dallas with purchasing agents from local hospitals or health care facilities needing to upgrade or replace their hospital beds. Even though Grant wasn't a born salesman, he did well because he wasn't pushy and had a gentle nature. He understood that people were interested in meeting an ex-NFL player, so he used that knowledge to his advantage. At six feet seven inches and north of 280 pounds, he still looked the part.

I didn't see how a move closer to DFW benefited him. He could run into a traffic jam anywhere on the expressways and freeways that crisscrossed the Metroplex.

"Do we really need to move?" I asked. "Think of all the disruption to the kids. We'd have to take them out of Dallas Christian, leave their friends . . ."

Grant held up a hand. "I just think it would be good for us to start over. A fresh beginning."

Then I understood. He wanted to put some distance between himself and my family. He wanted to live without family looking in or making judgments.

But the idea made no sense. We had a nice four-bedroom, three-bath home in a great family neighborhood, and I believe we had no problem affording that house. Everything was close by—a community swimming pool, shops and supermarkets, the kids' school, and my family—and we were getting to know our neighbors. I liked Rockwall—a nice, unpretentious middle-class community.

Nothing was settled, at least in my mind, but over the next month or two, Grant looked for ways to bring me over to his side. He settled on this pitch: "We'll buy a brand-new house. It will be our dream home. We'll find a great school for the kids, and they can stay in that school until they graduate."

"What's wrong with Dallas Christian?" I thought the kids were receiving a great private education in a Christian atmosphere at DCS.

"Nothing, except that I need to be closer to the airport."

Grant would not be deterred. He went house hunting on his own when he was out in the field. One night, he came home all excited about Colleyville, which was *west* of DFW and an hour's drive from Rockwall— and fifty minutes west of my parents' home in Garland.

"A realtor has been taking me around Colleyville," he said. "It's a hot place to move to. The model homes I saw were awesome, and many come with home offices. Since I work at home most days, having a home office would be another good reason to move."

I knew the Dallas area pretty well, having grown up there, but I didn't know where Colleyville was. The reason I was clueless was because this community of thirteen thousand sprang up in the shadow of Dallas/Fort Worth International when the airport became a major hub in the 1980s. I soon learned that Colleyville attracted upper-middle class families with a median household income of well over $100,000.

I had no desire to live in such an upscale area. Rockwall felt like a broken-in pair of slippers—comfortable and warm. New and fashionable Colleyville felt like the unknown. When our son Sean heard that we were looking at homes in Colleyville, he got upset. He had lots of friends in his fourth-grade class and loved his school.

Grant had an answer for that objection. He said that he'd heard that Fort Worth Christian School, close to Colleyville, was a great place to send your kids.

The new homes that Grant was looking at were at least double the cost of our home in Rockwall. "Shouldn't we be talking about moving into a more economical neighborhood?" I asked. "What about looking closer to Dallas Christian, which would put us nearer to the airport like you want?" If Grant was dead set on living closer to DFW, we could move a bit more west without disrupting the kids' schooling or our membership at Saturn Road Church of Christ.

Grant shook his head. "Nope, not going to work. We'll move into the house we want, and that will be the house we will live in forever."

Grant's mind was made up. I couldn't get him to budge. Although something didn't feel right about this move, he was the leader of the family. I let him make the final decision—a decision that would haunt us the rest of our lives.

CHAPTER 13

DOWN BY CONTACT

After I agreed with Grant's idea to move to Colleyville, we looked at new developments and chose a five-bedroom, five-bath home on a cul-de-sac in the neighborhood of Caldwell Creek. The house was still under construction, which meant we could put our personal touch on the finish work—countertops, cabinets, and flooring—when we signed on the dotted line.

At 4,485 square feet, our new home was certainly an upgrade from Rockwall: Grant would get his own office with a built-in library; we would appreciate his-and-hers walk-in closets in the master bedroom; and we would enjoy living in a home with two family rooms, a formal dining room, a game room, a laundry room, a gated entrance to the driveway, and a three-car garage. The backyard was a dirt patch, but Grant talked about putting in a big pool for the kids.

It was easy to get caught up in the excitement of "moving on up" into a grander home with all the bells and whistles and eleven hundred additional square feet. I believe the price was $400,000, twice that of our Rockwall home. Fortunately, our old place sold quickly at a good price, but we had to live in a Residence Inn for two months until our new house was finished.

In the coming years, Grant's decision to move us to expensive

Colleyville would put us under incredible financial stress, expose the growing divide in our marital relationship, exacerbate Grant's drinking problem, increase his addiction to painkillers, and eventually lead us into a very dark place.

In hindsight, I believe this is the time when chronic traumatic encephalopathy (CTE) began triggering progressive degeneration in Grant's brain tissues. I say that because the Grant Feasel I married—the peaceful, easy feeling guy—was rapidly changing into a mean-spirited and abusive person I barely recognized. His actions would propel me into years of therapy, suffering from post-traumatic stress disorder (PTSD) because of what happened with Grant in Colleyville.

The financial stress of owning a home we couldn't afford was overwhelming.

When we moved to Orchard Hill Court, our old furniture barely filled half of the house. The bedrooms were okay, but we needed a new couch for the main living room, a coffee table, an end table or two, a pair of lamps, and a new table and chairs for the formal dining room. In addition, we could have used a new dining table and chairs in the kitchen area. Another interior decoration necessity was window coverings—blinds and curtains. Many of our windows opened to the street, so it bothered me that neighbors could see into the house.

When I explained to Grant that we needed window coverings and more furnishings, he turned me down.

"We can't buy anything," he said. "You're going to have to hold off."

"How come?"

"Sorry. We can't do anything until I get another big commission check."

Meanwhile, Grant sought three bids for a backyard swimming pool. I thought we should get the house squared away and then worry about a backyard pool, but Grant didn't see things my way. The pool was nonnegotiable because of the kids, he said. When I saw that he wouldn't budge, I told him I preferred a small pool with more yard, but Grant wanted a big pool with a smaller yard. I lost that battle too.

The next thing I knew, a swimming pool contractor and his crew were digging a massive hole in the backyard for a gigantic pool deep enough for teenage cannonballs off a diving board. A separate spa was part of the plan as well.

We lived in a sparsely furnished house with a nice pool and spa in the backyard for the next year until Grant finally gave me the approval to do a "little" furniture shopping.

"Just be reasonable," he said.

I asked him what "reasonable" meant. I was told that I could purchase one end table and two lamps. That wasn't nearly enough furniture, but I figured that was a start. I worked with a decorator who was friends with the builder. She suggested several suitable pieces that I liked, so I gave her my Citibank Visa credit card number over the phone. When the decorator attempted to charge the card, however, the transaction didn't go through.

Embarrassing. I asked Grant why our Citibank Visa card was no good.

"I don't know," Grant blustered. "There must be something wrong with it."

I just had one credit card from Citibank Visa in my wallet. I rarely used it because Grant didn't want me to. I relied on a checkbook when I shopped for groceries or purchased clothes for the kids. But I never knew how much money was in the checking account because Grant wouldn't tell me. I wrote checks and hoped there was enough money in the checking account.

One time I drove to Albertsons supermarket. I wrote a check out for my grocery purchase and handed it to the cashier. She punched in some numbers and scanned the check. "Sorry, ma'am. The check's no good."

"Really?" My face turned red. Once again, I felt mortified as my groceries were packed up and placed in a shopping cart that was pulled off to the side. I drove home feeling extremely upset.

Grant's explanation? "I didn't know there wasn't any money in the checking account." He had enough cash on hand to allow me to return to Albertsons to pick up the groceries, but what happened bothered me greatly.

That night, before Grant went into our bedroom to relax with his "Diet Cokes," he handed me an American Express card. "If you're going to use this card, you have to let me know before making any purchases," he said.

This was so unsettling. It wasn't long before I got a phone call from American Express notifying me that this card was in arrears and we were being sent to a collection agency.

I hung up and waited for Grant to come home from work. After describing the phone call, I asked, "How come we're not paying on the card?" Grant wasn't even making the minimum payments.

"I'm working on that," he said. Then he offered an excuse. "They charged me for something they shouldn't have, so we can't use that card anymore."

One day, I happened to get the mail when Grant was out of town. There were two statements in the mail from Citibank Visa. I didn't know that we had *two* different credit cards from Citibank. The identical letters notified us that we were over the $10,000 limit, and since Grant hadn't been making the minimum payments each month, our credit was being cut off. Oh, and we needed to pay off the cards immediately or be sent to collection.

"What's going on here?" I demanded. "No wonder we can't buy furniture."

"Things will get straightened out when I get some money in a few weeks."

Again, I was in the dark about how much Grant was earning or when he'd receive his next commission check.

A couple of days later, Grant found me in the kitchen. He was holding a new credit card in his hand. "Here, use this, but only after you've cleared it with me." It was another American Express card.

"Why am I getting another American Express card when we can't pay off the other American Express card or our Visa cards?" I thought it was a fair question.

"I got a solicitation in the mail, so I called in and got the card. It's turned on and ready to use."

This was getting crazy. "Grant, how bad are our finances?" I asked.

Grant refused to answer, so I tried a different tack. "What if I help you with the checkbook so that we don't bounce any more checks?" We were bouncing checks all over town, including the kids' school. One of the rubber checks was super embarrassing: I bought a knickknack at a Fort Worth Christian fund-raising auction that I paid for with a fifty-dollar check that wasn't any good. I'll never forget a school mom calling me and saying, "I've been dealing with school families for years and never had a check bounce until yours."

When I asked Grant if I could help out with the checkbook, he looked at me and smirked. "No, you'll just mess things up. I know you too well."

"I can get a calculator and do the checkbook," I said cheerfully, doing my best to ignore the barb. I had a checkbook in college, and while I didn't like doing the math or keeping track of the ledger, I managed to not write any bad checks.

"Nah," Grant replied. "You can't imagine how many bills we have and how I have to juggle everything. Forget it. I'll handle things. You'll just mess things up even more."

The condescension was overwhelming. I would find out later that Grant had paid a moving company $10,000 to pack us up and move us fifty miles, had given a $15,000 loan to a friend with a gambling problem (that was never paid back, of course), and took out a separate bank loan to pay for the construction of the swimming pool—and stopped making payments to the bank. Eventually Grant even stopped making our mortgage payments and we lost our home to foreclosure. Meanwhile, he continued to pay for family trips to California several times a year, with stops at Disneyland, Sea World, and Knott's Berry Farm, activities we weren't even close to being able to afford.

Years later, I said to my sister Lori, "Why didn't anyone in the family say something to us when we sold our home and moved to Colleyville?"

Lori replied, "Because we thought Grant was an ex-NFL football player who could afford anything he wanted."

So did I.

TURNING THINGS AROUND

The move to Colleyville was the start of what I call the "strange and surreal" period of Grant's life. I was becoming more and more flabbergasted by the way he was talking to me. The put-downs were constant, and his belittling manner denigrated me at every turn. We could not have a civil conversation unless the kids were around.

This was so unlike the Grant I knew in the early years of our marriage. I missed the soft side of him, a sweet guy who strummed Eagles' songs on his guitar and felt vulnerable enough to sing to me. Now he was always on my case for just about anything and everything, especially our precarious financial situation.

We got into it one night after the kids were down. I'm not sure what precipitated the conversation, but it was probably about how the credit cards weren't working.

"Grant, something isn't right here. I just need you to tell me what it is. Why did you think we needed to move to Colleyville and buy a house this size?" I asked. "We could have bought a home closer to Dallas Christian or even Fort Worth Christian and lived in a very nice home. We could have paid cash for a house like that and not have these debt problems."

Photo courtesy of Cyndy Feasel

The eldest of three daughters, I was born and raised
in Garland, Texas, a leafy suburb of Dallas.

Photo courtesy of Cyndy Feasel

Grant grew up in the Mojave Desert in Barstow, California,
midway between Los Angeles and Las Vegas. He started
playing organized football when he was eight years old.

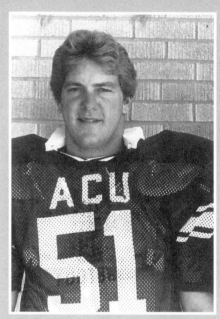

Photo courtesy of *Abilene Reporter-News*

Grant and I met after our third year at Abilene Christian University in Abilene, Texas. I thought he looked like a Greek god with his helmet of blond hair.

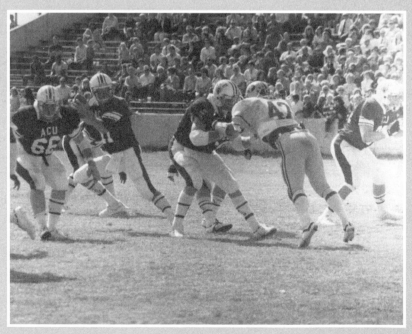

Photo courtesy of Cyndy Feasel

Playing center wasn't a glory position. Grant, shown blocking No. 42, used his size and power to protect the quarterback from attacking players.

Grant was a premed major at Abilene Christian who wanted to become a dentist. He also loved music and playing the guitar.

Grant rarely drank alcohol in college, but this changed when his NFL career ended and he sought relief from the effects of the battering his body took.

Grant and I were married on January 8, 1983, just a few weeks after Grant graduated. He was accepted into every medical and dental school in Texas, but the NFL thought he had the size and athletic ability to become a dominant center.

Photo courtesy of Corky Trewin

Grant, drafted in the sixth round by the Baltimore Colts in 1983, didn't play much during his first season before being picked up by the Minnesota Vikings in 1984.

Photo courtesy of Corky Trewin

Photo courtesy of Corky Trewin

After a serious knee injury during a Vikings practice, Grant worked hard in rehab and was picked up by the Seahawks for the 1987 season. He lost count of how many concussions he received on the football field.

Grant possessed the "warrior" mentality needed to survive and thrive in the "Not for Long League"—the NFL. He started fifty consecutive games over a four-year period and was the first player in the locker room every morning and last out every evening.

Called the "Fighting Feasel" by his teammates, Grant often came
home with battered fingers and scratched knuckles from his scrapes
in the trenches, which is why his uniform was often bloodied.

Grant loved it when our first child, Sean, joined him on the sidelines after games. Sean also saw up close his father's tremendous work ethic. Standing behind them is Grant's father, DeWayne.

Our oldest child, Sean, is four years older than Sarah and nearly ten years older than Spencer, and everyone enjoyed family trips to places like Tijuana, Mexico. Grant gained more than thirty pounds during his ten-year career in an effort to withstand the massive collisions that are part of playing in the NFL.

Photos courtesy of Cyndy Feasel

Grant and I struggled to maintain happy public faces in the years when Grant was in the throes of alcohol addiction and a dependence on pain medications and antidepressants. He was searching for relief from the aches and pains in his head as well as in his neck, back, and knees.

Photo courtesy of Cyndy Feasel

Grant's decision to move us from an affordable home in Rockwall, Texas, to a 4,485-square-foot home in Colleyville, wrecked our finances and caused our home to be lost to foreclosure during Grant's last year of life.

Photos courtesy of Cyndy Feasel

It was difficult keeping the family together in the last few years of Grant's life, when we didn't know his liver was giving out from excessive drinking.

Photo courtesy of Cyndy Feasel

My last photo of Grant is of Spencer and him at Spencer's high school graduation in May 2012. Grant, hospitalized for more than a month from complications of liver disease, rallied to attend. His health quickly deteriorated, and he died on July 15, 2012, while under hospice care. I am still devastated by the loss.

Grant leaned back with a smug look. "It's your fault we moved here. You're the one who wanted to move into a big new home like this."

"That's not true! You know it's not—"

"You had to have this house. You got what you wanted because nothing else was good enough for you. You wanted a fancy new kitchen and a game room for the kids and all those extra bedrooms."

I was incredulous. Grant was putting the blame onto my shoulders. "I was quite happy living in Rockwall," I said. "You said you needed to be closer to DFW because of all the flying you'd be doing. Don't you remember saying that? Now it turns out that you're flying a lot more out of Love Field, which means we didn't need to move in the first place."

Grant glared at me. "How was I to know about Southwest Airlines?" he said. It turned out that any time Grant wanted to fly to Houston, Austin, or San Antonio, Southwest Airlines had the best schedule, the most nonstops, and the cheapest fares, but Southwest flights departed from Love Field, Dallas's original airport located a few miles northwest of downtown and closer to Rockwall than DFW.

Seeing that I had punched a major hole in his argument that we *had* to move to Colleyville, Grant tried a different tack.

"We wouldn't be in this mess if you didn't buy so many clothes for yourself and the kids," he said.

I was a bargain shopper. I hunted for good deals wherever I shopped, from department stores like Dillard's to off-price places like Ross Dress for Less. The days of mink coats from Neiman-Marcus were long gone— though Grant would regularly bring up that purchase.

"You had to have that mink coat," he'd say over and over. "That mink cost us $5,000, and now you never wear it." The coat cost a fifth of that amount, but Grant ignored the truth—a quickly developing trend in our relationship.

Once he accused me of spending a thousand dollars at Ross Dress for Less, and even the kids laughed at that. "Dad," Sean said, "if Mom spent a thousand dollars at Ross, she'd be Customer of the Year!"

One day Grant found me in his closet and went ballistic.

"What are you doing in my closet?" he yelled. "I told you not to stick your nose into my business!"

"All you do is drink when you come home from work! You're drunk half the time!"

Something snapped in Grant. He suddenly pressed his big right hand on my chest and shoved me. He was still strong as a mule. I tumbled into a folding chair that he kept in the closet and spilled onto the carpeted floor, which was a sea of dress loafers and Nike sneakers. I was catching my breath when Grant slammed the door, leaving me totally in the dark.

Did this really just happen?

My hand hurt. I had broken a nail when I was pushed into the folding chair. This was the first time Grant was physically abusive with me. As I gathered myself, I knew I was going to get up and walk out of the closet, but I was afraid he would be waiting for me on the other side of the closet door. I began crying, then picked myself up and cautiously exited the closet. Grant had left. I walked out to the kitchen, saw the kids doing their homework, and never said a word about the ugly incident to them or anyone else.

I didn't speak to Grant for a week. I never even made eye contact with him. He said nothing about it, as if it never happened.

A GALA TO REMEMBER

We had lived in our Colleyville home for a couple of years when Grant asked me if I would accompany him to a hospital fund-raiser, a gala event held in a fancy hotel ballroom. Grant had bought a table for ten on behalf of Hill-Rom and invited several doctors and key hospital personnel and their spouses to join him. Grant felt it was important that I accompany him since the social gathering could become an important deal-making event for him.

Hospital galas are dressy occasions, so I wore a formal black evening dress. Grant dressed in a tux. A valet took our car in front of a luxury hotel in downtown Fort Worth.

It was a long night: enjoying a three-course meal—salad, entrée, and dessert; listening to long-winded speeches; taking in a live auction; and tapping our toes to country artist Larry Gatlin. Wine was served the entire evening.

I noticed early on that a bottle of red was stationed in front of Grant, and I wasn't keeping up with him. After refilling the glasses of his guests, he'd pour himself a refill. Ten, twenty minutes later, he'd do the same thing. And then another bottle of wine would appear in front of Grant. By the time Larry Gatlin came on, his guests said they'd had enough. Not Grant. He kept right on pouring.

At the end of a long evening, we stood up to leave. Grant looked like a California redwood about to topple to the forest floor. When he started walking, it was apparent that he was drunk. This was the first time I'd ever seen him stagger from drinking too much.

I sidled up to him. "Grant, you have to get ahold of yourself. You're drunk."

"No, I'm not."

Grant wasn't very convincing. I worried what would happen if he collapsed. Could I keep him on his feet? No way. Grant was a huge man. If I tried to keep him from falling, he would hurt me.

I tugged on his elbow and steered him to the hotel lobby. At the valet station, one of the uniformed attendants said, "Whoa, someone had too much to drink."

Grant laughed it off and handed him our ticket. As soon as our Suburban drove up, I took action. "I'm driving home," I announced as I escorted my drunken husband to the passenger's side.

Grant was too tipsy to protest. As soon as we pulled away from the hotel, my anger got the better of me.

"What happened tonight? Don't you know how you looked in front of all those people, many of whom are your clients?" I was furious and embarrassed.

"Shut up," he said. "Just get me home."

I was driving on a highway when he said, "I'm fixing to be sick."

I sighed. "Okay, let me pull over."

I drove onto the highway shoulder and rolled down his automatic window from the driver's side. Grant leaned out and unleashed a geyser of vomit.

"Feeling better?" I asked when he was done heaving.

"Get me home," he said.

The car smelled like vomit. I ignored the odor as best I could and steered back on the highway. We were only another mile down the road when Grant suddenly remembered something. "I lost my glasses," he said.

"How?" I asked.

"When I threw up."

I reversed course and found the same spot. Grant was too out of it to help, so I parked the car and looked in the dark for his glasses. There they were, sitting in a pool of vomit. I reached and grabbed his dirty frames. I couldn't believe I was doing this.

That's when I noticed vomit streaked on the passenger door panel. I couldn't take the babysitter home with our SUV in this condition.

I was now beyond furious. And Grant was passed out in his seat with flecks of vomit on his chin.

When we got close to the house, I drove into a self-serve car wash. It was after midnight. I got out of the car. I took off my black heels and hiked up my long black dress, tucked it in, and knotted it. In my bare feet, standing in soapy water, I triggered the high-pressure spray wand toward the vomit-splashed Suburban.

As we neared our street, I pushed Grant in the shoulder to wake him up. "This is what we're going to do," I said. "You're going to walk straight through the kitchen right to our bedroom. Do not make eye contact with the babysitter. I'll take her home."

Somehow, Grant followed my directions. I thanked the babysitter, gave her a generous tip, and then drove her home in a car that reeked of vomit.

She never said a thing.

I had a few things to say to Grant the following morning, however. "I can't believe how embarrassing you were last night," I said. "I sure hope the people you work for at the hospital didn't see you in that condition."

Grant smirked. "Please. Like it matters. Other people were drinking last night."

This was Grant's first public intoxication. In coming years, there would be many more incidents of him staggering in public, slurring his words, and falling to the ground and hurting himself.

We continued our pattern of fighting. Even though we were at each other's throats most of the time, the kids never heard us fight. We only raised our voices and pointed our fingers when the kids weren't home or were outside playing, or when we were behind closed doors in our bedroom.

To the outside world, we were all smiles and looked like one big happy family.

But that was so far from the truth.

INTO THE CLASSROOM

The financial pressures and never knowing if the next check would bounce to the ceiling or the next swipe of a credit card would be rejected wore on me.

One afternoon, while picking up Spencer from preschool, an obviously pregnant preschool teacher waved me down. "Cyndy, I'm going on maternity leave soon, so I'm looking for a long-term sub. I think you'd be perfect. What would you think of filling in for me? We can make sure that Spencer is in your class."

I didn't have to think twice. I had thoroughly enjoyed my year as a first-grade teacher in Abilene, and the sudden thought of getting back into the classroom excited me.

"I'd love to sub for you!" I was thrilled with the idea of shaping little lives. I'd be teaching at my kids' school, so how perfect would that be? I also appreciated the opportunity to make some money on my own and not have to ask Grant if it was okay to write a check at Albertsons. I opened a separate bank account under my name, but Grant was a signatory, meaning he had access.

Not only was the timing great, but I was also working the same hours that the kids were in school. I enjoyed my time in the classroom so much that I began thinking about what it would be like having a full-time job teaching at Fort Worth Christian. There was a powerful financial incentive as well: the children of teachers received a 75 percent discount on tuition. But I didn't tell anyone of my interest.

When I was done with the long-term substitution stint, the lower school principal called me into her office to ask me how things went. "Weren't you an art major?" she asked.

"Yes, I was. I have a master's in art education and love teaching children," I replied. "I'd like to get back into the classroom full-time someday."

The principal listened. "We have an opening for an art teacher. Would you like to join our faculty?"

I was so excited that I nearly jumped out of my chair. "I'd love to teach art! Just tell me when I have to start."

Once again, I said yes without talking to Grant about it, but I figured he'd be as happy as me. We needed more money, right?

Grant didn't show a reaction when I told him, although I thought he would have been ecstatic to hear that our tuition bills had been lowered by 75 percent.

"Are you sure you really want to get into something where it's every day? Because you don't really have to," he said.

Really? One of our recent checks for Spencer's preschool had just bounced.

"This is something I want to do. I want to use my education."

"You know that we're going to have to pay more taxes because you're working," Grant stated.

But that's because we're making more money, I thought. *A nice problem to have.*

I didn't care what Grant said. In the years to come, the only time I felt like a decent human being was in front of a class of wide-eyed kids who loved me.

CHAPTER 14

CHASED OUT OF THE POCKET

The period from the late 1990s to 2010, the year Grant's father died, was when Sean, Sarah, and Spencer came of age and the man I loved made life so difficult that I struggled to keep my heart open to him.

This was the era when, I believe, the repetitive brain trauma caused by the blows to the head he took on the football field triggered progressive degeneration, which, in turn, hastened his escalating addiction to alcohol and painkillers.

The changes happening in Grant's brain greatly impacted our three children and who they are today as adults. Their father's lifestyle decisions, erratic behavior, and extended withdrawal from their lives were devastating in many ways.

It's my greatest regret that they had to grow up in such an unstable environment, but I was flying blind and coped as best I could. I didn't know about CTE or how to navigate my way through many awful stretches and painful episodes. I still loved my husband, though, and hoped that eventually things would turn around.

Grant was most engaged with the family when the kids were gathered around the dinner table. If we happened to find ourselves alone, such as on a date night or celebrating an anniversary, we usually ended up fighting due to the alcohol. We got to the point where we couldn't communicate without arguing about the predominant role that booze was playing in his life.

After our date nights faded away but we still wanted to get out of the house, we took the kids with us to local restaurants. Their presence kept us focused on "safe" topics: the kids' school and athletic schedules; the social calendar; and future trips, like whether we would visit Grant's parents in Carlsbad during the next school break.

There was a lot of coordinating during the 2000s since we generally had at least one child in high school. Sean and Spencer played football and other sports, although football was their favorite sport by far. Grant, who'd coached the boys when they played youth football in middle school, attended every high school practice he could when his sons played for Fort Worth Christian. (The FWC coaches liked tapping into Grant's expertise.) As for Sarah, Grant enjoyed watching her cheerleading and running track during her middle school years.

During this decade, I veered into my "micromanaging" stage. In my misguided way, I was trying to help. My thinking was this: *If I can discover where Grant is hiding his stash of alcohol, then I can slow down his drinking—or put a severe crimp in it. And if Grant stops drinking so much, maybe our marriage and family life will get better.*

I looked everywhere for his bottles of booze. I constantly smelled for alcohol on his breath in the evenings. I rummaged through his medicine cabinet or bathroom drawers in search of painkilling medications, hoping to confront him with fresh evidence that he was medicating himself again.

Every time I micromanaged Grant, checked up on him, or moved a step closer to catch a whiff, he would hurl abuse at me.

Who do you think you are? I don't have to ask your permission to pour myself a drink. I don't have to ask you if I can take a pill. This is none of your damn business. Leave me alone, you stupid b——!

After laying into me, he'd take off for the neighborhood liquor store. Then he'd find a new place to hide his alcohol.

His home office became protected territory. Not only were there nooks and crannies among the shelving and cabinets, but Grant knew I couldn't rifle through his drawers when he was present. A floor safe that Grant had installed when our house was built further hampered my hunting expeditions. In addition to keeping important papers, the strongbox contained a stockpile of prescription painkillers.

Around 2004, Grant displayed the first outward signs that his body was rebelling against the onslaught of alcohol. Grant had been drinking daily for more than a decade. Sometimes he sipped Crown and Cokes to get a light buzz after dinner, but on other occasions he got hammered.

The alcohol was starting to interfere with his brain's communication pathways, which impacted the way his brain worked—a reflection of what CTE does. These disruptions caused changes in his mood and behavior, making it harder for Grant to think clearly and move with coordination. In addition, his heavy drinking was weakening his heart muscles and taking a toll on his liver.

I was at Fort Worth Christian after school when I received a frantic phone call from Grant.

"I'm in the car," he said breathlessly. "I think I'm having a heart attack."

"Oh no!" I exclaimed. "Should you be driving?"

"I'm trying to get to Baylor Grapevine as fast as I can." Grant was referring to Baylor Regional Medical Center about five miles from our home.

I couldn't talk Grant into stopping by the side of the road and calling 911. "We're coming now!" I yelled into the phone. Fear gripped my heart.

I gathered up Sarah and Spencer and headed to the hospital. Sean drove himself and met us there. We found Grant lying in a bed in a screened-off emergency room ward. An EKG determined that he wasn't having a heart attack. When it was apparent that Grant was going to be okay, the kids left with Sean.

I remained with Grant until an ER doctor returned with additional test results.

"From what we're seeing, your heart checks out clean, Mr. Feasel," the young doctor began. "It looks like you had an anxiety attack. I have a question for you: Do you drink a lot of caffeine?"

Grant shrugged his big shoulders. "Yeah, I suppose so."

I wish Grant had volunteered *how much* caffeine he consumed every day because it was off the charts. He started with a cup or two of caffeinated coffee at breakfast. Later in the morning or early afternoon, he'd stop by Sonic for a Route 44 cup filled to the brim with Diet Coke.

A regular twelve-ounce can of Diet Coke has forty-six milligrams of caffeine, which is judged to be a moderate amount of caffeine in a single serving, but when Grant was drinking a Route 44, he was consuming more than three-and-a-half cans of Diet Coke. When he finished his Big Gulp serving at home, Grant refilled his cup throughout the rest of the day and into the night with at least two more six-packs of Diet Coke, or 144 ounces, taken from our second refrigerator. When you add it all up, Grant was drinking roughly two hundred fluid ounces of caffeinated beverages, or sixteen cans of Diet Coke daily.

You could say that he had an addiction to caffeine as well as a dependence on alcohol. It must also be noted that Diet Coke contains aspartame, an artificial sweetener that depletes serotonin, a neurotransmitter in the brain responsible for mood swings, anxiety, and depression. I wish I had been aware of the health ramifications of drinking diet colas with artificial sweeteners at the time.

"You might want to stop drinking caffeinated drinks altogether," the doctor said. "In fact, I'd highly recommend that you do that."

Grant nodded. "I'll think about it."

The ER doc scribbled some notes. "Since it appears you had an anxiety attack, I'm writing you a prescription for Xanax."

Xanax was an antianxiety medication, which meant more mood-altering pills that Grant could hoard. Then again, Grant had a lot to be anxious about, like making sales, bouncing checks, and Sean's looming college bills.

Sean was starting college in the fall of 2004. He'd been a defensive back at Fort Worth Christian and wanted to follow in his father's footsteps—at Abilene Christian. Sean was enrolling at ACU and going out for the football team as a walk-on.

When Grant got home from Baylor Grapevine, he decided to follow the doctor's advice. He switched to drinking Diet Sprite, a caffeine-free diet soft drink. I would imagine the new taste took some getting used to, but Grant—and I—noticed that Crown Royal and Jack Daniel's didn't hide very well in the clear lemon-and-lime-flavored soft drink.

Grant had to do something. Vodka, he determined, fit the bill. Odorless and colorless, vodka packed the same alcoholic punch as a fine malt whiskey: both were eighty proof. I know that Grant settled on Absolut Vodka because I started finding bottles in his closet and office, which would prompt more heated arguments between us.

FACE TIME

Years of being on Grant's case took its toll on our relationship. As soon as the dinner dishes were cleared away and the kids went to their rooms to do their homework, Grant didn't want anything to do with me or have anything to say to me.

At the time I couldn't grasp what I had done or why he was acting this way, although I blamed the alcohol. I began to feel like I was a failure as a wife as he pushed me further and further away.

One night in our bedroom, I approached him. "My parents called, and they were wondering if we—"

"I don't want to talk to you, and I don't want to answer your questions," he said. "Your voice hurts my head. It's like nails on a chalkboard. I can't stand listening to you."

And then he took a couple of steps toward me, outstretched one arm, and covered my face with his right hand for a *long* time. My heartbeat increased sharply, not knowing what was going to come next. Was he going to smash me in the face at any moment? I didn't know. Grant was still a big man, and he could wipe me out with one backhanded swing of his arm.

He wasn't done. "Your voice bothers me. You're like a court reporter. You remember everything I say and use it against me forever."

This type of unpleasant behavior happened more and more frequently. When he wasn't intimidating me in this fashion, he made belittling comments about my weight:

If you weren't such a fat b——, then maybe I'd be interested in you.

Shut up, you fat b——. I don't want to listen to you.

This was extremely hurtful to hear because throughout the 2000s, I *was* fat. I never lost the baby weight from Spencer's birth in 1994 and was more than fifty pounds overweight. My clothing sizes had progressed from a size six to a size fourteen.

Given those developments in our marriage, physical intimacy became as rare as a blue moon. I'm talking about months in between. I didn't have any desire to make love because Grant always smelled of alcohol when we kissed. It was hard to get excited about being intimate when I'd been denigrated by a hand stuck in my face, told that my voice was grating, and regularly called a "fat b——."

I'd wait until he was asleep before going to bed, and then I'd stealthily crawl under the covers and try not to wake him up because I didn't want anything to do with him. Another reason I was careful not to disturb his sleep was because he could start drinking again—which could provoke another argument.

At our twenty-fifth wedding anniversary in January 2008, the problems with our physical relationship came to a head. We hadn't been lovey-dovey for a long time, but since it was our silver wedding anniversary, the expectation was that we should do *something* since we were still married. We drove to the Texas Hill Country and spent the night at a nice resort outside of Fredericksburg.

I don't know how we got through the white-tablecloth-and-candlelight dinner without having a major blowup. There was definitely tension in the air because we both knew what was building: the expectation that we would make love that night. We'd been married twenty-five years, right?

We returned to our resort room. We were both on edge, knowing what was coming next. Grant opened the only playbook he knew: having an adult beverage. "I can make you a drink," he said. "There's some cranberry juice in the refrigerator."

"I'm not going to drink vodka."

Even though we did it, the evening was a bust.

A few months after our twenty-fifth wedding anniversary, Grant tried again, but he couldn't perform—an issue that had happened in the past. I remember saying to him, "Have you talked to your doctor about your problem?"

Grant's family physician was a woman—Dr. Karen Shepherd (not her real name).

"What problem is that?" Grant asked.

"You know what I mean."

Grant grimaced. "At my last checkup, she asked me, 'How are your man parts?'"

"And what did you say?"

"I said they're fine."

"But they're not fine, and you know it."

Because of the way our love life was going, I had done some online research about the correlation between alcoholism and impotence. There sure seemed to be a strong connection. Alcohol is a depressant, and heavy use can dampen mood and decrease sexual desire, among other things. He would be impotent for the rest of his life.

There were other signs of physical decline. His wavy hair thinned and turned from a sandy color to dark brown, and his hair texture changed. The more he drank, the skinnier he got. His clothes hung on him like a scarecrow. His eyes got scarier. By that, I mean that his facial features sunk and his eyes became beady.

He also developed a stutter. He stammered as very unusual speech patterns emerged. He'd tell long, lengthy stories around the dinner table that might or might not be relevant to the discussion that was unfolding, prompting sideways glances between the kids and me. When he got a smartphone and started texting, some messages made no sense. E-mails were all over the map. He couldn't complete a thought.

I recall getting a phone call from a college friend who'd just gotten off the phone with Grant, who was out of town.

"Has Grant had a stroke?"

My heart sank. "No," I replied. "Why are you—"

"Because I could barely understand anything he said. He just rambled on and on."

Around Thanksgiving in 2009, we met my parents at a favorite Tex-Mex restaurant for dinner. Grant had been drinking that afternoon. He wore ill-fitting sweats and a jacket that hung on him. His face was ashen. That night, Grant talked nonstop to my parents, stammering every now and then.

My father knew something was terribly off, but he and Mom kept their thoughts to themselves.

I didn't confide my fears to them either. I was, however, looking to God for hope and for answers. I started sharing my innermost thoughts in my journal, thoughts such as these:

Please, God, show me the way. I need Your help. Take away the anxiety I feel. Help me to turn all my problems over to You, God. Keep my eyes on You and the cross where You died and took all my sins with You there. You know my heart, God, and the pain I feel.

My journals—I filled several volumes before Grant died—were where I could pour out all my troubles, prayers, and heartaches to Jesus. A scripture that resonated with me was from Matthew 11:28–30, where Jesus said, "Come to me, all of you who are weary and carry heavy burdens, and I will give you rest. Take my yoke upon you. Let me teach you, because I am humble and gentle at heart, and you will find rest for your souls. For my yoke is easy to bear, and the burden I give you is light" (NLT).

I did my best to cast the burden of Grant's deterioration onto the Lord's shoulders, but dealing with him had become as heavy as his towering physical presence. The only time I felt any solace was in my prayer time and my journal entries.

ANOTHER TRIP TO THE ER

Grant had another major health episode in 2009. It was Christmas Eve in Colleyville, and Grant had been in terrible pain all day. He was rolled up in a ball on his bed and couldn't straighten his legs out.

This was the second straight day that Grant hadn't gotten out of bed. His parents were staying with us, so there was concern on everyone's part that something was seriously wrong with Grant. While I was preparing dinner, Grant called out from our bedroom, which was on the ground floor off the kitchen and family room.

I went to see him. His wan, pale face didn't look good. Normally when he drank, his cheeks were flushed.

"You look like you're in a lot of pain," I offered.

"My stomach really hurts," he barely whispered.

"Do you need to go to the ER?"

163

"The ER has to be a zoo on a night like this. Can you see if Dr. Ramin can take a look at me?"

Dr. Ramin (that's his first name) was our next-door neighbor who was an emergency room doctor in Fort Worth. He and his wife had two children younger than our kids. We never had them over, nor were we invited into their home, but we were friendly to each other.

I hustled out the front door and ran across the yard. When I knocked on the door, I was in luck: Dr. Ramin answered.

I described Grant's symptoms and how much pain he was in. "Do you think you could take a quick look at him?" I asked.

Dr. Ramin smiled. "No problem. Let me get my bag."

I left Grant's bedroom while Dr. Ramin examined Grant. When I came back in, our neighbor said, "If Grant came into the ER, I would diagnose him with diverticulitis because he has all the symptoms, especially constipation. He's in a lot of pain."

"What's diverticulitis?"

"Diverticulitis is small, inflamed pouches lining the digestive system and is likely in the lower part of the large intestine," he said. "There's no cure for diverticulitis. The only thing we do is manage the pain with pain medication. I would also recommend that Grant stop eating seeds. That seems to help."

Grant perked up. "You mean sunflower seeds?"

I knew Grant really enjoyed eating sunflower seeds—and spitting out the shells. He said he liked to eat them during long driving trips in Texas and Oklahoma because they kept him awake.

Dr. Ramin nodded. "If you want to feel better, don't eat them anymore. I'm going to give you a prescription for pain medication to ease your discomfort and get you feeling better. As for the constipation, you need to drink lots of water. Very important. When the holidays are over, go see your family doctor. Maybe you need testing."

I thanked Dr. Ramin profusely as I walked him to the front door.

Then I drove to the closest Walgreens to pick up the prescription for Percocet.

Grant took one of the meds when I got home and remained in bed. I happened to check on him a half hour later when I noticed a Route 44 cup in his hand. That could only mean one thing: he was drinking Diet Sprite and vodka while on a painkiller.

"Are you mixing pain medication with vodka?" I asked, incredulous.

Grant blew me off. "Can you leave me alone? I didn't ask you to come in here and give me a lecture about my health."

I could get nowhere with him. Grant did surprise me, though, when he agreed to see Dr. Shepherd, who agreed with the diverticulitis diagnosis. She pressed Grant to have a colonoscopy, which revealed a few polyps but nothing that explained what was causing Grant all his pain.

In hindsight, Dr. Shepherd didn't have all the information she needed. Grant never told her that he was a daily drinker, which is why she never knew that Grant was developing serious issues with his liver and digestive tract. She didn't know to look. So why didn't I call Dr. Shepherd and tell her what was going on?

I tried to. I phoned Dr. Shepherd's office and asked to speak with her, but I was forwarded to a nurse. I begged the nurse practitioner to listen to me, but she said that due to HIPAA privacy laws, she couldn't discuss Grant's health or give me any information.

Later, I told Grant that I had called Dr. Shepherd, which turned him angry. "If I want you to know about my doctor visits," he said, "then I'd ask you to go along. I don't ask you if I can come to your doctor!" My hands were tied, but Grant got what he wanted: more pain medication to add to his collection.

After the brush with diverticulitis, Grant flew to Austin to make a sales call. He spent the night in a Courtyard by Marriott hotel and really must have had a bender because he was still drunk when he woke up for his early morning flight.

Grant somehow made it through airport security, but as he approached the gate, he made a scene. I guess it's not hard to miss someone who is six feet seven inches tall and totally out of it in the departure lounge.

The gate attendant denied Grant boarding because he was too drunk. Grant didn't take kindly to that. While ranting about the injustice, he slipped and hit the ground hard. Airport security was called, and Grant was escorted to a holding cell.

Grant's cell phone broke when he fell, so he couldn't call me. After sobering up in the holding cell, Grant told airport security that he had a son living in Austin (Sean, following his graduation from ACU), so they told him to sit tight. At the same time, one of the airport managers recognized Grant's name from an internal document. This airport manager played football at Abilene Christian with my brother-in-law, Eddie, which is the only explanation for why the police were not called. The manager gave him a break.

Instead, Grant was allowed to call a cab, which returned him to the hotel, where Grant checked back in to sleep it off. Then the airport manager called Eddie and explained the situation. Eddie then called Sean, who went to check on his dad. The decision was made to have Grant fly home the next day.

I was shocked when I heard the news from Eddie and Sean. When Grant returned the next day, though, he acted as if nothing had happened, and we never spoke about the incident again.

He was more concerned that his phone was broken.

BOUNCING AROUND

That's how we rolled. I had learned to expect that *anything* could happen to Grant.

From the time of the diverticulitis episode to the death of Grant's father in early 2010, I never knew what the next day would bring.

Any time I used the word *rehab* in a sentence, Grant ran out of the room like I was scratching a chalkboard with fingernails again. He did not want help or to be helped.

Quit bothering me. I can take care of myself. I don't want to talk about it.

I didn't see how Grant could hold on to his job since his behavior had become so unpredictable. His post-NFL career in sales hadn't been the model of consistency. After working five years for Hill-Rom, Grant bounced around the health care industry and was now on his third job since leaving Hill-Rom.

Looking back, I'm amazed that Grant was able to hang on to gainful employment for as long as he did. He did have some good years. Each April when I signed our IRS 1040 tax return, the boxed numbers never made any sense to me, but one year I distinctly remember seeing the part where Grant made more than $200,000 in commissions. Where all the money went, I'll never know.

With so much financial uncertainty hanging over me, I was thankful that I could use the money I earned from being an art teacher to purchase shoes and clothes for the kids or big-ticket items that I thought we really needed but Grant thought we could do without. To give an example, while the kids were still at home, the air-conditioning unit on the second floor—where their bedrooms were located—stopped working. It's hard to describe how uncomfortable a summer in Dallas can be with no air-conditioning.

The cost to repair the upstairs air-conditioning unit was $10,000. Grant balked; that was a lot of money. I pointed out that we were comfortable on the ground floor—where the living room, our bedroom, and Grant's office were located—because we had air-conditioning. Meanwhile, it was an oven upstairs, and the kids were baking.

"Ah, they don't need air-conditioning," Grant said. His solution was to buy some cheap fans from Walmart. The kids naturally stayed downstairs as long as they could until they had to go to bed. Sleeping in eighty-degree heat wasn't any fun.

I decided that wasn't going to happen when the next summer came around. I saved and saved until I had $10,000 to call the air-conditioning man to come out. It took me more than half a year to put together that lump sum.

Meanwhile, we were continually bouncing checks, avoiding calls from collection agencies, and watching helplessly as our electricity and water services were shut off. I felt powerless as we spiraled further down.

Not even rehab could help, but that's because an abnormal protein known as tau was taking over Grant's brain. It created an awful combination of emotional extremes and abusive rages and impaired his ability to control his impulses or exercise any common sense.

What I didn't know at the time was that Grant was entering the fourth and final progression of CTE symptoms, according to the Mayo Clinic. The four phases or stages look like this:

Stage 1: Headaches, loss of attention and concentration.

Grant complained about his aching head toward the end of his football career and right through the first decade of his retirement.

Stage 2: Depression, explosiveness, and short-term memory loss.

I couldn't put my finger on it, but something was going on with him after he retired from the NFL. There were personality changes and signs that he was easily agitated with me. Grant was forgetful in matters large and small.

Stage 3: Decision-making dysfunction and cognitive impairment.

Grant used to study thick medical textbooks and grasp the material in a single read-through, but balancing a checkbook was now beyond him.

Stage 4: Dementia, word-finding difficulty, and aggression.

Grant had a stuttering problem and couldn't complete a sentence or express himself in the manner he used to.

Even though I wasn't aware of these four stages, I was conscious that

I was losing the man I loved. I wanted the old Grant back, not knowing that he was *never* going to be the same and would only get worse.

In the last few years of Grant's life, the physical and mental erosion from CTE and abusing alcohol and painkillers would speed up rapidly.

CHAPTER 15

GETTING PHYSICAL

For years I tried to plead, pressure, and even coerce Grant into entering a rehab facility. Every time I thought the timing was good to raise the topic, his standard reply was, "I don't have a problem!"

I begged Grant to get help, but when he ignored me, I was on my knees crying out to God. "I'm free-falling, and I need You to help Grant," I prayed. "Please help him. The darkness is closing in on me."

In early 2010, I happened to be in our bathroom one afternoon when I spotted a bottle of lemon-lime Gatorade next to his sink, but the "drink" inside the bottle looked to be watered-down, which meant only one thing: Grant had spiked his Gatorade with vodka.

I unscrewed the cap to have a smell. Yup, the faint odor of—

"What are you doing?"

I looked up and saw a menacing Grant.

"Just checking."

"Well, it's none of your damn business. I don't understand why you make any of my stuff your business. Your sink is over there. Why do you always come over here rummaging through my stuff? I've told you before: Leave my stuff alone. Stay away from my sink. Stay out of my closet. Don't touch anything you find."

Chastened, I was setting the Gatorade back on the counter when suddenly, he grabbed both my arms at the biceps and squeezed as hard as he could, his neck muscles bulging and his face red with fury. He squeezed hard and maintained strong pressure as he shook me. I sank to the tile floor, screaming, "What are you doing?"

Grant didn't let up. He continued to shake me as I gyrated on the bathroom floor to escape his viselike grip.

"I told you to quit messing with my stuff. I don't know what it's going to take. You're always trying to *find* something. That's what you love doing—going through everyone's closet, rummaging through their stuff."

"That's because you're always hiding alcohol!" I yelled back. "Are you crazy? Let go of me."

I couldn't break free of Grant, which prompted me to kick at his ankles like a wild donkey.

"Don't kick me in the knees! Stop!"

We wrestled for another ten, twenty seconds or so—him holding me at arm's length and me trying to land a kick to his legs. When I tired and lost steam, he let go and stormed off to his office.

I rose up and looked in the bathroom mirror. My hair was strewn about, and my face was flushed. I washed up and carried on, but I made sure I kept my distance from Grant after that.

The next morning, in the master bathroom, I looked in the mirror and was shocked: my arms were black and blue from the shoulder to the elbow. Humiliated, I put on a long-sleeved shirt to cover the bruises.

I made sure I showed my purplish arms to Sarah and Spencer, however. I felt the kids should know that our marriage had taken a turn into physical abuse.

Naturally, Grant and I never talked about it again, but a few weeks later, I was in the laundry room, on the phone with my sister Lori. I was talking about how Grant was drunk again that afternoon—when my husband came at me like a blitzing linebacker and grabbed the phone out of my hand. He shoved me as hard as he could into the wall, and I tumbled to the floor.

"Call the police! Call 911!" I screamed at the phone.

Instead of dialing 911, Lori phoned Sarah, who was upstairs. "Your mom is in the laundry room, and your dad is doing something to her. You better go down there," she told my daughter.

By the time Sarah arrived, Grant was gone. I lay in a heap, crying.

"What just happened?" Sarah got down on bended knee.

"Dad was going nuts. He shoved me into the wall."

"Lori said I should call 911. Do I need to do that?"

"No. He left." Getting the police involved wouldn't solve anything.

I wrote this in my journal:

Pushing me against the wall, rambling about everything. Cursing and rambling. Where is the man with integrity that I used to know? He's gone and has gone far away.

I got to the point where I needed a time-out. During spring break in April 2010, I took Sarah with me and we stayed with my parents for a week. Spencer hung out with the DiCaro family, who lived in our neighborhood. Joe and Laura DiCaro were fabulous parents of two sons, Will and John, so I felt Spencer was in good hands. Grant remained in bed with his Sonic cups on the nightstand, but he called me nonstop and sent me on a guilt trip for abandoning him in his "hour of need."

"You've left me when I need you most," he said. "If you were sick, I would take care of you. How come you left me?"

Grant was trying to make me feel bad for finally standing up for myself and giving myself a breather from the toxic environment that he had created. He was attempting to turn the emotional tables on me, which left me torn up, bawling and crying. I wrote this in my journal:

> I feel so much pain. I feel bad for Grant because he is alone, but I can't do anything else for him. He has refused all attempts to help him.

When Sarah and I came back home after Easter, I said to him, "Grant, you've got to get some help. You're telling me you're working, but you're not. I'm coming home from school and you have your light on in your office and it looks like you're working, but you're just lying in bed—just like when I left you in the morning. You've got to get help. I beg you, please."

It was like talking to a brick wall. Grant was adamant that he didn't have a drinking problem and wasn't going to a rehabilitation facility. He wasn't eating or getting any sort of nutrition. He couldn't drive most of the time because he was drunk. Then he did something really bizarre: he called a cab and checked into a nearby hotel for a week. Dressed in a gray tank top and matching gym shorts, all he took with him was a briefcase. "You can be gone a week, and so can I," he said.

All I could do was shrug my shoulders. After Grant returned, I happened to run into a church elder while I was getting some exercise. I had known Keith Shelton and his wife, Lana, since our Abilene Christian days. Keith was an elder at the Hills Church of Christ, located in North Richland Hills. We had been attending the Hills Church ever since we moved to Colleyville.

"How's Grant?" Keith asked. Just from the way he asked the question told me that he knew something wasn't right with my husband. That simple question was all it took for me to start crying.

I described Grant's constant drinking and how he wasn't getting out of bed to do much of anything except to refill his Sonic cup. "I don't know what to do," I cried. "I'm afraid he's going to die."

Keith asked several more questions and then offered to pray for me. When he was done, he said he would call me in the morning. "Cyndy, I'm going to do everything I can to help you," he said. I believed this godly man.

True to his word, Keith phoned me on my cell the next morning while I was at school. "I'm getting some people together, and we're doing an intervention tomorrow."

I was overjoyed. I had already checked out my options and called Grapevine Valley Hope, an alcohol and drug rehabilitation center that offered detox and the 12-step treatment program on an inpatient and outpatient basis. I called our insurance company, who informed me that Grant's health plan with Fujifilm, his latest employer, would cover the cost of rehab.

I informed Valley Hope that Grant could be arriving sometime in the morning. When I left for school the next day, I left a side door open for Keith and his friends to do the intervention.

I wasn't at the house when the team from church arrived, but they somehow got Grant checked into Valley Hope.

Grant was supposed to be in a twenty-eight-day program, but he left after seven days. I didn't know that he could walk out of Valley Hope anytime he wanted to, but Grant insisted on leaving early, saying he had to go to New York City on a business trip for Fujifilm. This was way too early. Grant looked skinny and sick, but he asserted that this was a must-go business trip.

I have no idea how he conducted himself in New York City, but I do know that his trip home was a disaster. Grant's flight was supposed to arrive at 10:00 p.m. at DFW. Sean, who was in town, said he'd pick him up, but we weren't sure exactly what flight Grant was on because we couldn't trust him to give us the right information. (I was thankful that Grant didn't have a car at the airport so he wouldn't drive home drunk.)

Sean and I waited at the house for a phone call from Grant. We were only fifteen, twenty minutes from DFW, so the thinking was by the time Grant reached baggage claim, Sean would arrive curbside to give him a ride.

Ten o'clock, and no phone call from Grant. A half hour passed, then an hour. Still no word from Grant. I tried his number many times. Something was really odd, and I got very concerned. Sean was calling from his phone too. By 11:30 p.m., I was distraught and worried sick that something had happened to Grant. I called American Airlines to make sure that Grant's flight had arrived. Yes, the flight was on time.

Finally, around midnight, Grant returned Sean's numerous attempts to reach him.

"Dad, where have you been?" my son said.

"Ah, my bags are lost. They have to be around here somewhere." His speech was slurred.

"But your flight arrived two hours ago. What do you mean your bags are—"

"They have to be around here somewhere."

"Dad, where are you?"

"I don't know."

The reason Grant wasn't sure of his surroundings was because he had been drinking before he got on the plane, continued drinking during the flight, and had likely stopped for a nightcap at an airport bar once his flight landed.

"Dad, I'm coming to get you. You go to the American baggage claim and stand out on the curb. I'll find you!"

Sean got in his truck and raced to the airport. For the next forty-five minutes, he circled the arrival area, looking for his father. He called him every five minutes, but Grant didn't pick up. Then Sean called to tell me what was going on, and I was as frantic as ever.

Sometime after 1:00 a.m., Sean spotted Grant sitting on a bench outside baggage claim. He swung his truck to the curb and hopped out.

"Dad, get in the truck! You have us all worried to death."

"Oh, hi, Sean." Grant didn't have a care in the world—or his luggage. "I'm waiting on a cab."

"No, you're not taking a cab. You're getting in my truck, and I'm taking you home!"

With that, Sean manhandled his drunk father into the truck and texted me that he was on his way home. I did a slow boil, and when they arrived, my anger erupted: "What in the world were you doing? I can't believe what you're putting us through!"

I didn't make much of an impression on Grant. The next day he acted like nothing had happened. He didn't even seem terribly inconvenienced by having to drive out to DFW and fetch his bags being held by American Airlines.

Meanwhile, Sean had driven up from Austin to see his father because while Grant was in rehab, Sean had received several messages on his cell phone from a collection agency. Something to do with an outstanding bill at Abilene Christian. But Sean had graduated several years earlier in 2008.

Sean called me, wondering what he should do. I discussed the situation with my dad, who said, "Call the collection agency and find out what the problem is. It's probably something serious."

When Sean contacted the debt collection agency, he learned some shocking news: he owed $25,000 for his last year of college. Apparently, Grant had been ignoring ACU's monthly statements for years. Those ACU bills were among a big box of unopened mail that I found underneath Grant's desk while he was in rehab. There were dozens and dozens of other unpaid bills and invoices—some as old as seven years. No wonder our utilities and cell phones had been turned off. We were also behind on our mortgage payments. (I also found seventeen bottles of Absolut Vodka—some empty, some full—around the house and in his car.)

Normally, students are not allowed to receive their diploma unless they've settled up with the business office, meaning they need to take out student loans so that the university gets paid. In Sean's case, ACU let things ride because of Grant's legacy as a football star. Sean was allowed to walk with his class and receive his diploma. When Grant paid no heed to the demands for payment of Sean's final year in school, the university turned the debt over to a collection agency that—after never successfully contacting Grant—turned their attention toward Sean.

And now my son was on the hook for $25,000. I felt devastated by the news, and it was a huge financial setback for Sean, who was starting his career in the drywall business in Austin. He called the ACU office, explained the situation, and made arrangements with the university to pay back the sum in monthly amounts. ACU agreed to take the past due bill out of collections so that Sean didn't get nicked on his credit report.

That's why Sean came home—to get a straight-up answer from Grant. The morning after picking up his father at DFW, Sean attempted to have a man-to-man discussion with his father. Sean wanted to hear what his father had to say for himself.

"How come I owe ACU $25,000?" he asked his father. "How come you didn't tell me that you weren't paying for my senior year?"

Instead of saying, "Yeah, I screwed up," Grant replied that he had no idea what happened. When Sean pressed him, he heard the usual litany of excuses . . . *I thought I paid this . . . there must be some type of billing error . . . someone at ACU messed up.*

Sean left our house as frustrated as I had ever seen him. "I can't get any answers out of him," he told me. "He has an excuse for everything."

INTO THE CLOSET

It was evident that Grant was going downhill quickly.

"Grant, this is ridiculous. You need to get back into rehab. Am I going to come home from school one day and find you dead?"

Grant gave me a wave of his hand and stalked off. To go back into rehab was to admit that he had a problem with alcohol. For whatever reason, he didn't want to get sober and didn't want to live sober.

I was certainly worried about what I would find each day when I came home from teaching school. My fears were confirmed one afternoon when I arrived and couldn't find him anywhere in the house. I immediately ran to the backyard, fearing that he had tripped and fallen into the pool and drowned. He wasn't there.

I ran back into the house, my heart racing. I called out for him, but I didn't receive a response. The only closed door was the one to his walk-in closet. That was where he had to be.

"Grant, wake up! Open up!"

I banged on the closet door, which was locked and didn't budge. I was sure my husband was lying dead inside the closet.

I was alone. I couldn't open the closet door, so I called 911 and frantically explained what was happening. In a matter of minutes, a pair of Colleyville Police Department patrolmen were knocking at the front door. I led them upstairs to the closet.

They called for Grant and got no answer. Just like in a cop show, one banged his shoulder against the door, and it popped open. There, in the darkness, lay Grant. He was totally naked. The two policemen rushed to his side and woke him up. They struggled to get Grant to his feet and seated on the folding chair in his closet.

"Here, put these on." One of the cops was holding a pair of shorts.

Grant reacted slowly. "If you say so," he mumbled.

"Look, sir, we would like to take you to the hospital," the other officer said. "It looks like you're going through a tough time. Can you tell us what's wrong?"

"Well, my dad died," Grant said. "I haven't been the same since. My wife isn't understanding, and she gets into my business. She's not a good person. She's always getting into my business."

The policeman turned to me. "Do you want us to take him to the hospital for a forty-eight-hour observation?"

I didn't see what a trip to the hospital would do except give us more medical bills that we couldn't pay. "No, there's no need to. He'll just come home and be more mad."

A couple of weeks later, I came home from school and found him in his office. He was watching a DVD made from a PowerPoint presentation he had made for a speaking engagement. Grant hadn't spoken before an audience—or been asked to—in years, but recently he had driven to Oklahoma to speak at a men's retreat. I know how Grant drove himself to Tulsa—just like he drove himself everywhere. He was a very cautious, hand-position-ten-and-two driver, knowing that he wasn't at the top of his game behind the wheel.

At any rate, Grant had prepared a PowerPoint presentation of his life . . . black-and-whites from his Barstow years . . . standing next to his towering father as an eight-year-old . . . playing at Barstow High . . . making a name for himself at Abilene Christian . . . action photos from Game Day in the NFL. There were lots of memorable photos of the kids growing up, including cute shots of kindergarten-age Sean hanging out in NFL locker rooms.

With a Sonic cup on his desk, Grant stared at the computer monitor as the photos from yesteryear clicked through. His eyes were watery; these visual mementos obviously meant a great deal to him.

This scene became a regular occurrence: I'd come home from school, and Grant would be watching that DVD. If I walked into his office, he always said the same thing: "I'm trying to watch this DVD that I have of my family! These pictures mean a lot to me!"

Each day he was flat-out drunk. This went on for a week, spending his afternoons with a DVD of family photos and action shots from the gridiron. I understood the sentimentality and how he loved his kids and was trying to relive nice family times we had together, but he was neglecting the world around him, including his work. How was he selling anything?

I figured he was on thin ice at work. I imagined that clients were calling Fujifilm and saying, *What's with this Grant Feasel guy? He's acting drunk and not all there.* Grant told me that HR was on his tail—whatever that meant—so he had to be feeling the heat.

All this history was swirling around my brain when I came upon Grant wasting another afternoon in front of his computer, watching the same DVD over and over.

"Are you drunk?" I demanded.

"No, I'm not. And if I was, what do you care?" Grant responded.

"What do you mean, 'What do I care?' You failed rehab and don't have any interest in getting sober. You went AWOL at the airport, and now all you do is look at pictures of yourself when you played football!"

"Get out of here, you b——!"

Something snapped. I looked for something to throw at him. Several family photos, resting in glass frames, were on his desk. I grabbed one and threw it like a Frisbee. I didn't want to hit him, but I tried to make sure my throw sailed right over his head. My aim was good. I flung the first frame of family photos above him, which hit a bookshelf, shattering glass. Then another, followed by another. And another.

"I hate you! I hate what you've done to this family! You've ruined our marriage, and you've ruined everything, including our kids! You're a drunk, and your drinking and pill taking have destroyed our family!" I stormed out of his office.

When I had a moment to calm down in the kitchen, I realized that flying off the handle wasn't helpful or loving behavior. The only good thing to come out of the incident was how it reopened the discussion about rehab. Grant agreed to return to Valley Hope, but there were no beds available, so he participated in the outpatient program. After a month, I noticed that Grant was coming home from rehab drunk.

"I thought you went to rehab," I said.

"I did, so don't bother me."

I was right to be concerned because Grant was given a Breathalyzer test at rehab. After flunking a couple of times, he was kicked out of Valley Hope's outpatient program. That left Alcoholics Anonymous as his last hope. He joined an AA class at Southlake, but he was still drunk most days.

Grant insisted on driving to his AA meetings even when he was tipsy. One rainy afternoon, he left the house in a really inebriated state. I fretted about his condition to Sarah, who offered to drive me to the meeting so I could bring Grant home.

When he came out, I asked him to hand me the car keys. He refused, which touched off a tussle. I fought him for the keys, but he was too strong and pushed me into a puddle. Then he jumped behind the wheel of his car.

Things got crazier after that. I pounded on the driver's side window while Sarah screamed and onlookers gawked. Grant got the car started, giving me a moment to yank open the door. Grant put one hand around my neck and shook me until I saw nothing but black. Just before I passed out, a male bystander yelled at Grant to release me. When Grant relaxed his grip, I stepped away from the car.

More words were exchanged when suddenly a cop car pulled up. Someone had called 911. The Southlake policeman took stock of the situation and asked me if I wanted Grant arrested.

"No, that's not going to help anybody. He really needs to be checked into Valley Hope," I said, referring to the rehab center.

"I can't have you get in the same car as him," the policeman said. "He needs to ride with someone else."

I pointed to my daughter standing next to her car. "Sarah can drive him."

The policeman herded Grant toward Sarah's car and assisted him into the passenger seat. As Sarah pulled onto the main thoroughfare, I followed—when suddenly Grant's door popped open and he stuck out a leg, like he was going to jump into the busy road.

Sarah pulled off to the shoulder. I came up alongside her car. Sarah rolled down her window and was hysterical. "Dad says he's not going!" she yelled. "And if I drive him to rehab he's going to jump out of the car!"

I was tired of fighting him. "Okay, take him home."

Out of sorts and out of ideas, I called his brother, Greg, after we got back to the house. "I don't know what to do with him anymore," I told Greg.

We discussed treatment options for Grant. Greg suggested an out-of-state rehab facility, a secluded place where Grant could get the help he needed, but that would mean a plane flight.

We agreed that Grant was in a too-weakened state to fly anywhere.

LOOKING TO GOD

These were dark, dark times. So where was I spiritually throughout this black period?

I was on my knees, saying, *God, I need You. I'm lonely.*

While I knew His love for me never wavered and that He knew everything that was happening to me, it was hard to deal with the disintegration of Grant and our marriage.

When I had a spare moment, I looked to the Bible for hope and camped out in Psalm 102, including the first two verses:

> God, listen! Listen to my prayer,
> > listen to the pain in my cries.
> Don't turn your back on me
> > just when I need you so desperately.

This passage was so powerful to me. I also wrote prayers out to the Lord in my journal:

> God, please help me to seek You first.
>
> God, please help me to listen for Your voice. Help me be better at arranging my life in the chaos and put You in the highest place every day! Help me be confident that You are always with me . . . and You know my needs. Help me to rely only on You and the Holy Spirit's strengths and powers.

I collected relevant Bible verses such as Lamentations 3:22–24 and Ephesians 6:10–12 and held them close to my heart. Psalm 56:8 was especially meaningful to me: "You've kept track of my every toss and turn through the sleepless nights, each tear entered in your ledger, each ache written in your book."

I firmly believed I was in a spiritual battle. Something had gotten hold of Grant along the way. When I met him he was a spiritual giant, just as he was a dominating physical presence on the football field. But fifteen-plus years of addictions had clouded his mind and thrown him off the straight and narrow path.

Looking back, I wish I had confided in family and friends—or sought help from a pastor—about Grant's wayward course, nightly drinking, and the abusive way he treated me. I was too immobilized and too scared to seek help or throw out a lifeline until I sought counseling in the late 2000s.

In the meantime, I poured out my pain to the Lord and coped as best as I could. I read my Bible for inspiration and guidance. A section of scripture spoke to me after I began seeing a therapist. It was 1 Peter 5:7–9, which reads like this:

> Give all your worries and cares to God, for he cares about you.
>
> Stay alert! Watch out for your great enemy, the devil. He prowls around like a roaring lion, looking for someone to devour.

Stand firm against him, and be strong in your faith. Remember that your family of believers all over the world is going through the same kind of suffering you are. (NLT)

Even though I read many times that the devil was looking for someone to devour, I never thought for a moment that person would be me.

CHAPTER 16

INTERCEPTION

At some point in the 2000s, I stopped staying in touch with my friends. Sure, I was wrapped up in teaching and caring for my kids, but life was easier when I let relationships fall by the wayside. If we didn't talk to anyone or go anywhere, then they wouldn't know how messed up our family was—or see the pain on my face. Nobody knew the truth about Grant's alcoholism or the abuse he heaped upon me. Not even my parents or two sisters.

Grant didn't cultivate friendships either and stopped calling his family. I felt that we should keep the communication lines open, so I would send e-mails and occasionally pick up the phone to call Pat or Linda to describe what the kids were up to or what was new in our lives.

One weekend in 2009, I happened to be chatting with Linda. Our conversation occurred at a time when I was depressed and binge eating to fill a hole in my life. I'd sit in the red chair in our family room and polish off an entire box of Triscuits while watching a mindless TV show. Big bowls of Blue Bell mint chocolate chip ice cream were another weakness. When I told Spencer one time that I was making brownies, he said, "Don't eat them all before I get home." His admonition was grounded in experience.

"I'm just so worn-out all the time," I told Linda. "I feel exhausted when my school day is over. I'm overeating and putting on weight. I don't have any energy or feel like myself." At the time, I was tipping the scales at 185 pounds, my highest weight ever.

Linda had always known me as an upbeat person who sought out the sunny side of life. "Why don't you go see a doctor?" she suggested. "Maybe there's a reason you're not feeling well. Perhaps you need to have some blood work done."

Linda had a good idea. I had started menopause and hadn't seen my "woman doctor" in a while. Maybe that's why I had a major dose of the blues. "I think I'll do that," I told her.

I made an appointment with Dr. Alan Unell at FEM Centre, a women's wellness clinic in Colleyville with a focus on relieving hormone-related health issues. I liked the way Dr. Unell and his colleagues treated women with natural remedies and bioidentical hormone therapy.

It didn't take long for Dr. Unell to realize that I was unhealthy in many ways. As he asked questions and compiled my patient history, I felt he was safe to talk to. I let down my guard and described what was going on in my life, from Grant's drinking to my lack of energy.

After I mentioned that I was seeing a therapist, Dr. Unell urged me to make several key lifestyle changes that would help me regain my physical health. He outlined the importance of preparing and consuming fresh foods and eating nothing out of a box or a can. I heeded his advice and started grilling meats instead of frying breaded cuts in grease. I stopped purchasing processed foods and serving my family fried chicken and mashed potatoes or heavy casseroles. Instead, I prepared hearty meals of barbecued chicken, grilled fish, fresh vegetables, and lots of salads.

I even bought a juicer and started juicing fruits and veggies in the morning. I made smoothies using a special protein powder from the wellness clinic and took certain vitamins. To treat my menopause symptoms, I took bioidentical hormones produced by Dr. Unell and his team.

Grant didn't know what to think when he saw me whipping up a morning smoothie and taking a handful of nutritional supplements. One time, he asked me, "What kind of quacky doctor are you going to?"

"I'm trying to turn my health around," I explained. "I want to feel better."

"Good luck," he said sarcastically.

The biggest lifestyle change championed by Dr. Unell was the importance of exercising. "When you work out, your body releases chemicals called endorphins that trigger a positive feeling in the body," he said. "Not only will you feel better, but you'll lose weight exercising and feel even better about yourself. I recommend that you moderately exercise for at least thirty minutes a day."

We had a family membership at LifeTime Fitness, a local health club, but I hadn't darkened the front door in ages. I decided to start exercising three times a week and see how I felt. I showed up for cardio classes, used weight machines, and walked on the treadmill, spending at least an hour working up a sweat. I found that exercising after dinner was most convenient for me, even though that meant a long day.

At first, Grant thought I was on one of my periodic kicks and that my newfound interest in fitness would be forgotten as quickly as a New Year's resolution in February. But as I pressed on, he used the opportunity to cut me down. "You never cared about what you looked like before now," he said. "Why are you trying to work out and get skinny? You've been a fat b——our whole marriage."

I used his cutting remarks as motivational fuel. I started exercising at LifeTime every weekday and even on weekends. The pounds melted off. I lost twenty pounds the first year and had to buy a whole new wardrobe. By the end of 2010, I had lost more than forty pounds. I had been wearing "big and baggy" clothes for years to hide my flabby body, but now I could wear *tight* clothes. I remember standing in front of a full-length mirror at the club and thinking about how far I had come. *You're not a fat b——. You look as good as any other woman in this gym.*

Successfully losing weight helped me feel better about myself and made me happier. When I needed to exercise before work because of after-school commitments, I didn't mind getting up at 5:00 a.m. and breaking a sweat in the predawn darkness.

One morning, I was getting ready for my school day. I had packed a duffel bag with my exercise clothes since I planned to zip to LifeTime Fitness right from school.

Grant noticed me gathering my things before heading out the door.

"Where are you going?" Grant nodded toward my duffel bag.

"I'm going to the gym after my last class. I'm not coming home first because I have to turn right around and pick up Spencer." Our youngest son had football practice, and I was his ride.

I thought Grant's question was off the wall. I had taken a change of clothes with me to school on many occasions in the past year.

A month later, he saw me leaving the house with my duffel bag and asked me where I was going again.

"Straight to the gym after school."

"I don't understand why you don't come home and change."

"Grant, they have lockers. Lots of people go to the gym after work."

Grant paused for a moment.

"I think you're meeting somebody," he said.

Hearing him say that was incredibly hurtful—like he had balled up his fist and slugged me in the pit of the stomach. Why would he accuse me of seeing someone else behind his back? What he said to me was insane.

Perhaps he wanted to get back at me for recently moving into the guest room to sleep. I couldn't handle how he was up and down constantly during the night, making a racket in his closet, topping off his Sonic cup, bumping into walls, knocking over lamps, or falling onto the bathroom tile floor in his stupor. I needed my rest since I had a classroom of kids to teach.

"You're crazy," I said. "I'm going to the gym and working out. Then I'm coming straight home. You know that."

"No, I don't. I don't know what you do anymore. You tell me you're doing this and doing that. You're really not accountable at all."

I pushed back. "Well, I work all day, and when school's out, I'm usually at the gym or shopping for food and doing errands. I don't know how you think I could be doing anything else."

"Well, I just think that you *lie.*"

The venomous way he pronounced the word *lie* hit a nerve. *All I've ever done is to cover up for you and lie constantly to everybody about what you do. And you tell me that I lie.*

He wasn't done yet. "You're losing all this weight because you want to get skinny for somebody else. There's a man in your life. I know you're having an affair. I know you're sleeping with somebody."

Grant was living in some alternate universe. He also told me that he had been googling my name. "I've seen all sorts of pictures of you with different men on the Internet," he said.

"What are you talking about? You googled my name?"

"Yeah, I have. Wait until your dad finds out what you've been doing."

"This is crazy."

I turned on my heels and went to our home computer and googled my name. Looking under "Images," there were four or five headshots of me, mostly from the Fort Worth Christian faculty page. Not one photo of me with another man, including Grant. I guess I had never done anything Google-worthy, but that's how delusional Grant was becoming.

I should have excused his warped view of my world as a product of the alcohol, but I couldn't. Grant *wanted* to hurt me with outlandish accusations and spiteful words. That's the way his passive-aggressive personality worked; he didn't yell at me, but he sure cut me into pieces.

What happened was so unbelievable and depressing that I just wanted to stay at the gym and be as far away from him as I could for as long as possible. The longer I ran on the treadmill, the happier I was because the minute I came home Grant was all over me, ripping me constantly.

Did he ever say these things in front of the kids? Of course not. He made sure he spoke nicely to me when they were in earshot. But if we were in his home office or the bedroom door was shut, he would go on and on about how I was having an affair and had been two-timing him throughout our marriage and had even cheated on him before we got engaged. "And I still married you, to be nice," he said.

This was the time in our marriage that I compare to living in a mental institution, listening to a tape of him calling me a fat b——, asking me if I was seeing someone at the gym, and accusing me of having an affair.

There was no pleasing him in any way, shape, or form. He didn't like me fat, and he didn't like me skinny. He never told me I was beautiful. He never told me I was pretty. The way he treated me was so degrading and terrible. I don't know why I stood for it. I should have told him off and gotten in the car and driven away.

"I'm going to leave you because you don't love me," I said one night in our bedroom.

Grant chuckled. "You're not leaving me. Where would you go? Live with your parents? Really, Cyndy? You can't afford to live anywhere. You're a schoolteacher. You don't make enough to live on your own. The kids would never come live with you. Our kids want to have nice things, and they want to live in a nice house. They don't want to live in some nasty apartment somewhere. They don't want to go with you and live with your parents."

Our marriage was in tatters.

ACCEPTING A COMPLIMENT

One of the few constants in our lives was attending church on Sunday mornings. A ministry that Grant liked being involved in at the Hills

Church was volunteering at the welcome center as a greeter—someone who offered a friendly handshake and a booming, "Howya doin'?" to folks as they arrived from the massive parking lot. The Hills Church was a mega-church with thirteen thousand members, so lots of greeters were needed to say hello and point families to the main sanctuary and Sunday school classrooms.

By 2010 or so, Grant was showing up for his greeter duties on Sunday morning in a tipsy state. A couple of church leaders approached me and asked, "What's going on with Grant?"

At first, I made excuses for him, but it was apparent to the church leadership that Grant was half-drunk at 10:00 a.m. on Sunday mornings. It was a painful day when Grant was informed that he wasn't welcome to be part of the welcome center ministry anymore.

Grant really didn't want to go to church after that. I still wanted to go—I needed the teaching and the fellowship—but I needed a new church. I looked around and found Gateway Church, a multicampus nondenominational church in the Metroplex with a satellite location in North Richland Hills. I was drawn by Gateway's Equip program for those dealing with addiction issues and also for their phenomenal music. The worship pastor was Kari Jobe, a Christian recording artist and writer of "Revelation Song," a worship tune I adored.

Spencer continued going to the Hills Church because of his friends, but Sarah joined me at Gateway. Attending church without Grant was another loss in my life, although he did join me a few times. I wrote this in my journal:

> Grant is so far away, on an island, and I'm all alone. I want out. I want to die from what this feels like.

One Sunday morning after attending church by myself, I ran into an old friend. I'll call him John. He was a longtime acquaintance, but Grant and I had never socialized with him when he was married. I recalled hearing that he had gotten divorced several years earlier.

I saw John in the church foyer. I remember saying hi and then half joking, "Where have you been?"

"Where have *you* been?" he replied with a smile. It had been so many years since we had seen each other.

"Oh, around. I'm teaching at Fort Worth Christian. Grant's still in sales in the medical field."

"Where's Grant?"

I blew out a long exhale. How best to explain the unexplainable?

"You don't know anything about what's going on with me because I haven't seen you in so long."

"No, I don't know anything." John's open-ended comment seemed to open up a door. I was feeling like I couldn't protect Grant any longer. Before, he kept his drinking behind the four walls of our Colleyville home. But as he started drinking around the clock more often, he was prone to showing up half-drunk—at church, at Spencer's football practice, or at Friday night football games.

"Well, Grant has some addiction problems, and I'm struggling because of that. I'm at a point in my life that I don't know what's going on with him myself."

"I hate to hear that. That certainly doesn't sound like the Grant I used to know." John sounded pretty shocked.

Gee, he cares that I'm going through some bad stuff and having troubles.

As if reading my thoughts, John said, "Has anyone ever told you that you are a beautiful woman? I'm sorry for the heartache you've had because I can tell that it's been rough."

John reached for his wallet and handed me his business card. "Here's my phone number. If you ever want to talk, call me."

I thanked John and wished him all the best. He meant well, and I appreciated that.

I tucked his card inside my purse. Over the next couple of weeks whenever I saw that card, I thought of John's offer to have a chat. Maybe it would do some good to unload on somebody I didn't know very well.

But it was John's compliment that stood out in my mind—*you are a beautiful woman.* I never heard Grant say that to me, and if he had, then it happened during our dating days in Abilene nearly thirty years ago. Ever since Spencer was born, Grant told me that I was a "great mom" or a "great wife"—the roles he saw me in. Although I appreciated the compliments, they did not make me feel special to him.

I looked at John's card and then at myself in the mirror. *It's weird that somebody would say this to me when my husband never told me I was beautiful. Because I am beautiful to someone!*

I wrote this in my journal in March 2011:

> I saw an old friend at church. I'm thinking about meeting him for coffee. I need to get out of here anyway. Grant only loves vodka and pills, and I am not on his list of loves. He's been over me for years. I stopped being what he needed years ago. His need is vodka.

Two or three weeks after we met, I called John. "Hey, remember me?" I said over the phone.

"Yes, matter of fact I do. Good to hear from you, Cyndy."

"I've decided that I need some wise counsel. Can we talk?"

"Okay, when would you like to meet?"

"I don't know. When's good for you?"

"How about next Saturday morning? There's a Starbucks on Davis Boulevard. Shall we say 9:00 a.m.?"

Saturday morning seemed like the logical time. I taught during the week and Sundays were reserved for church in the morning.

The following Saturday morning, Grant was still sleeping off a hangover. Sarah and Spencer had friends over and had stayed up late, so they were still asleep. I remember having on jeans and a T-shirt and walking out the front door. I didn't say anything to anybody.

John was waiting for me. We found a table with our lattes. John immediately asked me about Grant and what had happened after football. I described all his knee problems and how he had gotten so banged up playing in the NFL that he medicated himself with alcohol and drugs. We basically talked about Grant for the entire hour.

It felt good to have an attentive ear. John had been the perfect listener. "Let's get together again," I heard myself saying. "This was fun."

"I'd like that," said John, opening the door as we left Starbucks.

Another two weeks passed until we met again on a Saturday morning. I initiated this rendezvous as well.

I talked more about my troubles with Grant and got emotional. John reached across the table and touched my hand, and I felt a jolt of electricity. Somebody was looking in my eyes and paying attention to me. A man hadn't touched my hand like that or looked in my face in a long, long time. Grant seemed to prefer to hold a hand in front of my face and remind me that he couldn't stand the sound of my voice.

Once again, I thanked John for being such a willing listener and promised to call him, which he welcomed.

A couple of weeks later, I phoned and made a date to meet at Starbucks again on a Saturday morning. We happened to drive into the parking lot at the same time.

"Good seeing you here," I said cheerily as I exited the car.

"And good to see you. I was thinking, why don't you just come home with me?"

I gasped and wasn't sure if I had heard right. "Instead of having a coffee?"

"Instead of having a coffee."

I wish I had thought about his indecent proposal longer. I wish I had thought through the ramifications of what he was suggesting more thoroughly. What he was proposing, however, sounded really good. A series of questions ran through my mind:

Who's this going to hurt?

Nobody because nobody cares about you. Grant has proven your entire marriage that he doesn't care about you.

Is there anything to lose?

No, because Grant doesn't love you anyway.

Why are you doing this?

Because you deserve this. You deserve something for all the hell you've been through.

Apart from the primary question about the moral considerations of his proposal—which were all-important to me, or at least should have been—there was another question that I should have asked myself: *Will anyone find out?*

I was too caught up in the moment to think that last one through. But I had been in so much darkness that hearing someone say, "You look beautiful . . . you look pretty," were the charming words I needed to hear. I was like a dry bone in the desert.

So I followed him to his house, feeling like I was on an adventure. When I crossed his threshold, I stepped into the world of adultery. What had started as an emotional affair turned into a physical one.

The entire experience was surreal. Several times I said to myself, *I'm not really doing this, am I?*

But I was. And I did.

I went back home that morning, acting normal. A couple of weeks later, John and I met up again, and it wasn't at Starbucks. It was at his house again.

When I got home, Grant found me in the kitchen. It was the early afternoon, and we were the only ones home.

"I want to talk to you," he said. Grant had been drinking already.

That sounded ominous. "About?"

"I want you to get in the car with me. We'll go to Sonic."

"I don't want to go to Sonic." I didn't drink anything at Sonic except for iced tea.

"I just want you to get in the car with me and drive around a little bit."

Oh my gosh. I couldn't think of a legitimate reason to turn him down. I got in the car, and Grant was acting weird. I could tell that he wasn't happy with me.

"I know what you're doing." The automatic locks clicked.

Why did I get in the car with him?

"I know exactly what you're doing."

"What are you talking about?"

"I know you're having an affair."

I did my best to keep a blank face. "You've been saying that I've been having an affair for years. So why do you say it like it's happening today?"

"I'll tell you why. I've been looking at the phone bill and the times of day you've been talking on your phone. I see that you've been talking to somebody late at night. And it's not me."

God, please get me out of this car. "Take me back home. I'm not going to put up with this, and I don't know what you're talking about."

"I'm going to find out who you're seeing. And why do you have a password on your phone? You never had one before now."

"Why do you care?"

"Because I think you're having an affair, and having a password proves it."

I vehemently denied the accusation, and we got nowhere. He drove me back to the house in a huff, but my heart was in my throat. *How did he find out?* I was really unnerved.

He continued to press me. I figured I had to give him something.

"Okay, the truth is I'm having an emotional affair," I said as we drove through a Colleyville neighborhood.

"Why would you need to have an emotional affair with anybody?"

"Maybe because you and I can't talk to each other unless we're fighting. You and I never do anything together."

"You never loved me anyway, you whore."

The conversation didn't improve after that. When we got home, doors slammed, and Grant locked me out of the master bedroom. I wasn't sleeping there anyway, but my clothes were there. Thankfully, I had hidden a small brass key to the bedroom door, so I could get to my clothes.

I kept my distance from Grant but still continued to see John on the sly for a couple of months, careful not to get caught or leave any tracks.

Then one Saturday when I met John at his house, he wasn't happy to see me.

"We're not doing this anymore," he said.

"What?"

"I don't feel right about this. You've got a lot of stuff to take care of. I've already been through a divorce—an ugly one—and this is not going to work out."

John looked relieved to break off the affair, but I was distraught. The pain of rejection was agonizing.

"You've got to be kidding!" I said. "This cannot be true."

"It's best we go our separate ways, Cyndy."

I begged him to reconsider in a jumble of tears, but he stood firm. I left his home devastated and feeling like a fool.

I managed to pull myself together by the time I pulled into our driveway. Even though John had blown me off, I continued to try to get in touch with him. I was emotionally unstable. I may not have been Glenn Close in *Fatal Attraction* crazy, but I was in the neighborhood.

This was a dark, dark time.

A pit in my stomach told me that this wasn't going to end well—for Grant or for me.

CHAPTER 17

SEEKING FORGIVENESS

After the affair ended, I couldn't feel anything anymore. I felt completely dead. I could have walked over hot coals and not noticed a thing. My nerve endings were seared.

My conscience wasn't seared, though. In fact, my soul was full of anguish because I knew I'd really messed up. I deeply regretted breaking my marriage vows that I had made to Grant and to God.

In the aftermath of the affair, I didn't run away from God, even though I was aware of many people who go off the trail like I did and say to themselves, *You know, I'm done with God.* Instead, I sought my heavenly Father with a heavy heart and trusted God's Word that He loved me even in spite of what I had done. I knew I had to ask Him for forgiveness, but I was in a very depressed and fragile state.

There were moments when I felt so low that I wondered if everyone would have been better off if I jumped into the deep end of our backyard pool and never came up again. Then I envisioned my kids seeing that and how that memory would stay with them for the rest of their lives.

In the midst of this breakdown, I felt that somehow Satan had gotten inside of me and won. It was like I had crossed over into a world where I didn't even know who I was. I didn't feel alive anymore, like I had died in some way.

How did I get to this point? How could I let this happen? After all those things Grant had called me, and all of the lies he had constantly said about what I had done, I finally did what he had been saying all along. I couldn't see how I was going to get out of my situation—it was that bleak.

In the midst of my pain and confusion, I gravitated toward the most comforting and encouraging passage in the entire Bible—Romans 8:39:

> I'm absolutely convinced that nothing—nothing living or dead, angelic
> or demonic, today or tomorrow, high or low, thinkable or unthinkable—
> absolutely *nothing* can get between us and God's love because of the
> way that Jesus our Master has embraced us.

I wanted to be in church the following Sunday. Pastor Robert Morris, at the end of an excellent sermon, said what he says every week: "I want you to bow your heads and close your eyes. What's the Holy Spirit saying to you? What do you need to pray about right now? What area of your life do you need the power of God released in? We want to pray for you. In just a moment, we'll have leaders in the front. If you need prayer for any area of your life, I want you to come to the front and let one of our leaders pray for you. There's nothing too small or too big to be prayed about." Slow piano music played in the background, lending to the emotional moment.

That's all the invitation I needed. I left my seat and made my way to the front, where I joined dozens of others at the front of the stage. Nearly as many members of the prayer team were waiting for us.

I met the gaze of a husband-and-wife couple. After asking my name, the husband said, "How can we pray for you?"

I had to gather myself for a moment. "I'm in a horrible place in my life and feeling closed in. I've done some terrible things and need to ask God for forgiveness. I have a broken marriage, and I have a husband who's an alcoholic and an addict. The alcoholism has come to a point where he's really bad and affecting our whole family. I'm desperate for you to pray for forgiveness for me and for God to turn his life around, and for my kids, who need him and need me."

The couple gathered around me, each putting an arm around a shoulder. The husband prayed first. "God, You know Cyndy's heart. You know she loves You. Forgive her of anything that's gotten in the way of her and You."

Then his wife chimed in. "Lord God, we're agreeing with Cyndy that she needs Your help. She knows that You're there for her and that You've never left her side. We're agreeing with Cyndy that You're going to help her find her way, that You're going to take care of her, that You're going to protect her, and You're going to lead her into a place where she knows the answers to all the questions she has right now. She's in a place where she doesn't know what's going to happen next, but we know that You will provide for her."

Tears streaming down my face, I confessed in my heart to the Lord that I was truly sorry for what I had done and asked for His forgiveness.

I departed Gateway Church letting out a huge sigh of relief and with clarity on what I needed to do. Grant's daily drinking over the course of many years had destroyed our love and our relationship. I was tired of being abused and called filthy names whenever the whim struck him.

When the new school year started, I knew it was time to leave Grant. I had seen a divorce attorney before the affair, and she had given me several tips, including going into Grant's office while he was out of town and taking pictures of bottles of vodka and documents that could bolster my reasons for leaving him.

I had been saying things to Spencer that were clues to my intentions. I voiced comments like "I don't know how much more I can stand" or "I don't know how much longer I can stay," which he shared with his brother, Sean. This prompted a phone call from my oldest son. When

I told him that I had been putting a lot of thought into leaving his dad, Sean urged me to reconsider.

"Mom, you can't leave until Spencer graduates!" he exclaimed. "You'd be a horrible mother if you left him during his senior year. Spencer is going to be graduating in May. That's going to be here so soon."

I was in a quandary. Sean had a point, but I didn't think I could last another year with Grant. I was in a severely weakened mental state. I wrote this in my journal:

> I feel so sad and lonely. I love my kids, but they can't take the place of the love I had for Grant. How did he slip so far away from me? I promised I'd love him until one of us died. I can't stand the pain anymore. It hurts like open-heart surgery without anesthesia. The pain is too deep! I want to die from what this feels like. I want out. I've got to find a way out. Help me, God!

It was one episode after another with Grant. There was the time when he attempted to drill into his floor safe because the key had broken off. He cracked several drill bits in a desperate attempt to get more painkilling medication. On another occasion when I was sleeping in the guest bedroom, he stormed in at 3:00 a.m., flipped on the lights, and brandished a large knife taken from a cutting block. He said he'd just called the police and told them I was trying to kill him.

I looked at the kitchen knife he was holding. "You said I was trying to kill you?"

"Yeah, I did."

"Grant, how could I kill you when I've been sleeping soundly in the guest bedroom?"

Grant hadn't thought of that. "But you want to!"

"No, I don't. Go back to bed."

Grant shrugged and left. Once I heard the master bedroom door close, I jumped out of bed and locked myself in the bathroom. I didn't know if he would be coming back—or what he was capable of in his mind-altered state. I hadn't forgotten how he squeezed my arms or choked me in front of my daughter, half out of his mind with rage. I was afraid of Grant, who constantly called me vile names and slammed doors in my face. No matter how frail Grant was, he was still bigger than me.

I gathered towels and lay down on the tile floor, curling into a ball and trying to sleep. The police never came, but the more likely story is that Grant never called 911.

Terrified, I wondered in the dark, *How did I get here?* I didn't know what to do and saw no way to navigate my way out of my marital mess. I prayed, "God, what have I done to deserve this? You know I'm so sorry for what I've done. I can't stand what my life has become anymore."

At the time, I didn't know about the connection between CTE and Grant's erratic behavior and his verbal and physical abuse. I was aware that the human brain is made up of billions of neurons that constantly coordinate every physical move within the body, but I wasn't informed of the relationship between those damaged neurons and his emotional state and threatening behavior.

Grant couldn't hide his addictions any longer. His secret was out. One morning, while doing errands, I dropped by the dry cleaners to pick up Grant's shirts. The lady behind the counter, before ringing up the bill, said, "Can I ask you something that's confidential?"

"Sure," I replied.

"What's wrong with Grant? He looks so bad and acts so strange."

I didn't mind being asked. In fact, I felt validated that someone had asked me straight-out what was going on with Grant.

"You're correct that Grant isn't doing well. He's working through some things. I appreciate your concern."

I felt like I was living in a fishbowl. I recognized the knowing glances from parents and teachers at Fort Worth Christian. I couldn't eat. Every time I took a bite of food, I couldn't get it down.

"I think you have anorexia," Grant said, meaning that in his eyes I had gone from being fat to someone who was too thin. "I've talked to your sisters, and I've talked to your dad, and everyone is worried about you because you don't eat anymore."

I wasn't sleeping very well. Since sleep came in spurts, I never woke up feeling rested. I was in a weakened state and dealing with a lot of anxiety. I was still teaching and doing okay at work, but I was scrambled in my thoughts.

I wrote this in my journal:

I'm numb most days, going to school, waiting for what will happen next and feeling mentally unstable at every turn.

One of the people who found out what was going on was a divorced mom named Lori Walker. Her son, Jamie, and Spencer were close friends. Jamie, who was a grade ahead of Spencer, had hung out at our house many times and had seen Grant drunk and witnessed a lot of bad stuff, which I'm sure he described to his mother. Jamie was attending Abilene Christian and was a tight end on the football team.

Lori reached out to me, and I confided in her. During the summer of 2011, she said, "I couldn't have made it through my divorce if somebody hadn't helped me. The least I can do is help you. I'm going to be coming and going for the next year, so if you feel like you absolutely have to leave Grant, please take my place. I live in a nice duplex. There's room for Spencer, so don't worry about Jamie. He'll be in Abilene preparing for the football season."

Hearing Lori offer her place gave me hope. I now had someplace to land when I jumped off the ledge.

Shortly after school started in August 2011, I came home after the last class and threw some clothes and an armful of family photos into my car. That's all I took. I had maybe a thousand dollars to my name.

Grant was gone. I placed a set of divorce papers on his desk. I had told Spencer, who was at football practice, that I was leaving Grant and said he could join me if he wished. Lori's duplex had two bedrooms.

"Nah, I don't want to," he said. "I feel like somebody needs to stay here to take care of Dad, but I understand why you're going."

We hugged. Both of our hearts were breaking.

I don't know how I successfully drove to Lori's duplex in nearby North Richland Hills because I could barely see the road from all the tears running down my cheeks. When I arrived, I immediately texted Spencer: Will you come?

His answer: No, I'm okay.

I heard from Grant at 10:00 p.m. that night.

"Where have you gone?" he asked. I could tell he had been drinking.

"Grant, I've left you. There's no reason for me to live with you anymore. You hate me. You've done nothing but try to get me to leave you for many years. You quit loving me years ago, and all you love now is vodka."

Grant pushed back. "You're a terrible mom. I can't believe you would leave Spencer like this! He's a senior this year. How can you walk away and leave him like he's nothing?"

"I'm not going to try to reason with you right now."

"Well, you can live over there if you want to, but I'm not going to divorce you."

"I don't care if you divorce me or not. I can't take the pain and the heartache from living with you anymore. You tried to choke me, for crying out loud, in front of our daughter! You threatened me with a knife! We have no life together. There's no reason for us to be living under the same roof."

And then I said good-bye.

I had told my principal at Fort Worth Christian that I was leaving Grant, and she and the administrative team expressed nothing but support. They had seen Grant at school events and knew he was a shell of his former self and incapacitated by alcohol. Spencer came to my classroom every morning before the start of school. I brought him breakfast—a homemade waffle, a Chick-fil-A bacon biscuit, or a Whataburger breakfast taquito. At lunchtime, I left campus and got him some fast food or a burrito at a nearby taco shop. Spencer gave me updates on Grant, but his reports were more of the same old, same old.

Grant continued to call me, saying more guilt-inducing things like, "I hope you're happy because we don't have anything to eat."

"Why would I be happy about that?" I asked, although I wondered why he couldn't go to the supermarket himself and buy some groceries, especially if he was hungry.

Being the enabler that I was, I did go food shopping—on my paycheck—for Grant and Spencer. I'd hand Spencer a half-dozen bags of groceries to take home so that they would have something to eat. I even prepared meals like lasagna and burrito casserole for them and gladly did Spencer's laundry. It was easy for him to drop off his dirty school and football uniforms since Lori's duplex was just two blocks from Fort Worth Christian.

I also made Spencer's truck payments because he had no money and neither did Grant.

A DIFFERENT COLOR

When I saw Grant at Spencer's football games, we had awkward conversations. He looked awful. His face was flushed and blotchy, and his skin was puffy and yellow.

Since our lives were out in the open within the Fort Worth Christian community, I'm sure we were the targets of gossip. I had done a good job of protecting Grant, but that wasn't possible anymore.

One Friday night, I was sitting in the grandstands watching the Fort

Worth Christian Cardinals football team play and keeping my eye on Spencer, who was a six-foot-two split end and defensive back who played both ways on offense and defense.

Suddenly, I heard a siren in the distance that kept getting louder and louder. Within a matter of seconds, a paramedic's ambulance pulled into the parking lot behind the FWC bleachers, prompting a lot of rubbernecking. Something must have happened.

Another team mom touched me on the shoulder. "Grant's fallen in the parking lot," she said.

I grabbed my purse and took off running. When I arrived, paramedics were tending to Grant, who was lying on his back. He couldn't move. It was evident that he had collapsed onto the pavement.

"I'm his wife," I volunteered.

"Do you know what medications he's taking?" asked one of the EMTs.

"He takes a lot of medications—Vicodin, Percocet—and anti-depressants," I said. "And he drinks."

The EMT met my eyes. "We can tell," he said.

I don't know why Grant was in the parking lot during the game or what happened to him. He must have lost his balance and fallen. He couldn't move.

I didn't follow the ambulance to the hospital. There was no point. I couldn't rescue him this time. Besides, what could I do? He was just going to go home and drink again.

Grant was held overnight for observation. No stitches—he was just banged up and bruised. A doctor looked him over and told him, "You need some help. You need to get into rehab. It's not too late for your liver. If you quit drinking, you could have more time."

More time to live.

I can only imagine what Grant's liver was like after eighteen years of nonstop drinking. Alcohol is a toxin, which the liver's enzymes must break down and eliminate through the digestive process. As the liver processes alcohol, it can damage the liver's enzymes, which leads to cell death. As cells die, scar tissue forms. This is known as cirrhosis of the liver. If excessive drinking continues, eventually the liver can become too scarred to function properly.

The liver can self-heal when the drinking stops, however, which is what the doctor was referring to. But long-term damage to the liver is usually irreversible, which was likely Grant's situation.

When I called Grant following his release, I asked him what happened.

"Oh, I got a little light-headed," he said. "I guess I fell."

The collapse at the football game was the first strong signal that Grant's liver was starting to shut down. After that, Grant began retaining water in the abdominal cavity, causing his stomach to bloat from the pressure buildup of fluids. In medical terms, Grant's stomach was distended. He looked like he was going to have a baby.

When the abdominal bloating was too severe and the pain too intense, Grant had Spencer drive him to the emergency room. Each time Grant underwent a medical procedure to drain the fluid buildup. As soon as Spencer took him home and he was back on his feet, Grant drove to the liquor store. He still needed his alcohol.

I visited Grant one time after he went to Texas Health Harris Methodist Hospital HEB in Bedford to have his abdomen drained. Afterward, I made small talk in the hallway with a nurse. "Your husband's lucky," she said. "If he was in a public county hospital, they would just let him die."

The drainage episodes were becoming more and more common. After the fifth one, Spencer called and asked if I could give Grant a ride back to the house. I said fine.

"Thanks for picking me up," he said as he gingerly took the passenger seat. "Can we go by Panda Express and get something to eat?"

Grant was in a mellow mood, and we enjoyed a pleasant meal. As we were leaving, I asked, "Is there anything else you need?"

"Yeah. Can we go to Sonic? I want a Diet Sprite."

While sipping his Route 44 on the way home, Grant said he couldn't understand something the doctors said to him. "They keep telling me my liver's shot, but they won't put me on a transplant list. I don't know why my doctors won't do that."

I looked at Grant. "You continue drinking and expect to get a liver transplant. That's not going to happen."

Grant stared out the passenger window and then turned to me. "I guess you're right," he said in a near whisper.

THE DISSOLUTION

In between trips to the hospital, our divorce became legal sometime in March 2012, seven months after I filed. Grant, in typical fashion, dragged his heels as long as he could. He called when everything was said and done.

"I hope you're happy now since you've destroyed our family," he said.

"Grant, I'm never going to be happy about what happened. I can assure you that I'm devastated over this. I'm never going to be the same."

I didn't think divorce was okay. I had grown up in a family where there wasn't any divorce. That's why I stayed with Grant for so many years; I didn't want a black check mark against our family name. Even though I didn't want to get a divorce, it was foolish for Grant and me to continue living together. I couldn't live in the same house with someone who was drinking himself to death and regularly calling me a b——and a whore.

There was very little to divide; we had very few assets. Our Colleyville house was in the midst of foreclosure because Grant had stopped paying the mortgage a long time ago. The only reason the bank hadn't booted him and Spencer out of the house was because the Dallas-Fort Worth area was working through a backlog of foreclosures stemming from the recession of 2008. Since the bank hadn't gotten around to the eviction process, Grant was living rent-free.

As for me, I was living in fear of the Repo Man. I was driving a Ford Edge, and Grant hadn't made loan payments in months. Any day I expected to come out to the school parking lot and see a tow truck hauling away my transportation. Plus, I was receiving harassing phone calls and texts from Grant telling me to bring back his car. I spoke about the situation with my dad, who offered to help me get a new car. I dropped off the Ford Edge at the Colleyville house with the keys in it, and then Dad drove me to a local Honda dealership, where I leased a new Honda Accord.

There was one other "asset" to discuss—an asset now worthless. Grant at some point had stopped making payments on a $2 million life insurance policy. When the kids learned of this, they were understandably devastated.

I didn't blame them. They could have done a lot with that tax-free money: pay off college bills, start a business, buy a house. Grant's decision to stop paying on his life insurance policy and thus leave nothing behind for his children was unconscionable.

Sarah was very upset that her dad was dying and no money would be available for her to finish college and get a start on life. She approached her father in tears for an explanation.

"Dad, what happened to the life insurance? What are we going to do?" she asked, crying and sniffling.

"Why are you crying about the life insurance?" her father replied. "Is that the only reason you love me—because of the life insurance?"

Once again, Grant skillfully made it sound like she was at fault. Sarah, so delicate, was devastated.

RAPID DECLINE

In April, Grant's health took a turn for the worse. His mother, Pat, flew out and took charge. Grant would never be able to live alone again and needed someone to care for him and make adult decisions.

I got the message very quickly from Pat that she thought I was the root cause for everything: the divorce, Grant's rapidly declining health, and the financial mess. She believed my decision to abandon him had pushed him over the edge and caused him to start drinking heavily. I was responsible for his recent free fall into illness, and because of that, she deeply resented me. Since Grant had accused me of cheating on him with many men, I would imagine he shared the same accusation with his mother. He painted me as an unfaithful woman of low character who had wronged him in the worst way possible.

And now her son was dying because of me.

Looking back, it's clear that nobody in Grant's family knew what Grant and I had been through. They didn't know he'd become an alcoholic and a drug addict after retiring from the NFL; that was well hidden in the united front that Grant and I presented to the world. In the absence of that knowledge, Grant's family made their own judgments, having no idea what our marriage was like behind closed doors or how Grant had acted toward me all these years. Instead, I felt like they viewed me as a modern-day Hester Prynne, the Puritan woman required to wear a red A—for adulteress—on her dress in *The Scarlet Letter*.

The next time Grant had to go to the hospital to have fluid drained from his abdomen, Pat asked me to leave when I arrived for a visit. "I just think you're making Grant upset," she told me.

"Pat, I was married to Grant for twenty-eight years. He's the father of my kids! I've been coming every day, and he hasn't seemed upset to see me at all."

I started visiting Grant after 10:00 p.m., when I knew Pat wouldn't be there. I saw him every night. Our visits were cordial, tender, and even welcomed. There were tender moments when I fed him applesauce or Jell-O with a spoon. He wasn't upset to see me and was glad I was there. He knew he was facing his mortality, and we both put the past in the past.

Grant rallied and was able to leave the hospital one last time to see

Spencer graduate in late May. My parents and I met him and Pat, along with Spencer, at a Mexican restaurant beforehand. Seeing him in his black suit shocked me. He was skin and bones in a suit that could have wrapped around him twice. His neck was a stick in his shirt. Liver disease had taken this big man down to nothing, and he would never get better. Reeling from the revelation, I sat down next to my parents and gathered myself.

We sat in the same row at Harvest Christian Church for the graduation ceremony. Grant didn't have the stamina to stand and talk to anybody when graduation was over. At a time when everyone was supposed to be happy and optimistic about the future, there was so much sadness. We didn't get to celebrate Spencer the way we should have.

Since Grant and I couldn't afford to send Spencer on a graduation trip, we breathed a sigh of relief when the parents of a school friend invited our son to join them for several days in Cancún on the Gulf of Mexico. That trip was scheduled for after the Fourth of July.

Meanwhile, I continued to visit Grant each night in the hospital. Toward the end of June, I asked Grant if I could lie next to him in his hospital bed. He nodded his approval.

I saw his DNR bracelet on his left wrist—Do Not Resuscitate—and shuddered. The years passed by in a flash. Standing before my dad and family and friends, we had given our lives to each other, for better or for worse, for richer or for poorer, and in sickness and health till death do us part.

Till death do us part. I held my breath because we were on the precipice of that day.

As if reading my mind, Grant took my hand and looked in my eyes, which were wet with tears. "I'm sorry for what I've done to you," he said, and he meant every word.

His simple sentence of contrition jolted me. I had never heard him say he was sorry for what he put me through.

"Thank you," I managed. "I'm sorry too. This is not the way we wanted it to be."

Grant exhaled, as if he wanted to get something more off his chest. Then he uttered the most profound sentence I ever heard him speak: "If I'd only known that what I loved the most would end up killing me and taking away everything I loved, I would have never done it," he said.

There wasn't anything I could say or add to what he said, because in a few words, he had said it all. Grant had made amends, and that released me.

We had a moment. I felt lighter than I had felt in years. Then a thought and a prayer came to mind: *Please, God, don't let him die without talking to all of the kids and asking for forgiveness from them.*

I planted a light kiss on his cheek, said good-bye, and returned to Lori's apartment crying and feeling so sad. *He's going to die. He's really going to die!*

Shortly thereafter, on a July evening, I heard from Sarah that Grant was being moved the next morning to VITAS hospice in downtown Fort Worth. The news of Grant's final journey left me in shambles because that meant my visits were coming to an end. I figured that it would be impossible to see Grant at the hospice since access would be more tightly controlled at an end-of-life facility. This evening would be my last chance to see Grant on this side of heaven.

I asked Keith and Lana Shelton, our friends from college and the Hills Church, to accompany me. I needed support at a traumatic moment like this. When we walked into his hospital room, I was greeted by a surprise: Grant's eyes were open and clear, revealing a pure green pigment. Gone was the darkness. Grant's eyes hadn't been that clear in years!

Grant had a pair of plastic tubes inserted into his mouth, so he couldn't speak. I held his hand and cried, knowing that I was close to losing him. Grant tried to say something but couldn't. "You don't have to talk," I whispered. "Grant, I'm not going to be able to come to the hospice center. I'm saying good-bye to you here."

Grant blinked his comprehension. Before we left, Keith uttered an emotional prayer that God would be close to Grant and be with him every step of the way.

I left the hospital feeling like we were at peace.

I never saw Grant alive again.

CHAPTER 18

THROWN FOR A LOSS

In the early morning hours of July 15, 2012, a Sunday, I was awakened when Sarah called me at 7:00 a.m.

She was hysterical. "Mom, it's Dad! Mom, it's Dad!" she exclaimed.

"Sarah, stop. You've got to breathe so you can tell me exactly what's going on."

"Dad died, and I wasn't there."

A profound sadness came over me, but I was also grateful that Grant's final journey had not lingered. He'd been transferred to VITAS hospice just five days earlier.

"Sarah, your dad was going to die whether you were there or not."

"Yeah, but I wanted to be there. I just left to get some rest."

My daughter explained that she had been staying at Grant's bedside around the clock but left the hospice just before dawn to grab a few hours of sleep. She was staying at our house in Colleyville and calling me from there. She told me she was alone; Pat and Linda had remained at Grant's side. When he took his last breath, one of them called Sarah with the sad news, which is why my daughter was phoning me.

"Sarah, that's okay that you went home. Dad probably waited to die until you were gone. You did everything right, believe me."

"I'm going back," she said, sounding relieved. "I need to be there."

I wanted to accompany her to the hospice because this was a time for family, but I knew I wasn't welcome. I desperately wanted to give my daughter a hug—and receive one from her.

"Okay," I said. "If you want, I can meet you at the Quik Trip gas station at the corner of Mid Cities and Davis," I said, referring to the intersection of two major boulevards in North Richland Hills.

Sarah had been brave and strong during Grant's final days. She'd been by her dad's side every step of the way.

When we met at the gas station, I squeezed her tight and didn't feel like I could let go.

"Mom, will you go with me?" she asked.

I sighed. "I don't think it would be good for me to join you. I think it'll be good for you to be there, so go."

I wished her all the best as she drove off. I wondered if the boys had heard the news. Sean was on a fishing trip in the Gulf of Mexico that had been organized by his work. Spencer was in Cancún with a couple of school families. I decided that it would be better if they learned of their father's death from Sarah or Pat.

Grant's funeral was five days later on Friday, July 20, at the Legacy Church of Christ in North Richland Hills. I arrived that afternoon with my parents and immediate family—my two sisters and their spouses. We were lingering in the foyer when Pat and Linda approached us.

"We're going to have you and your family sit across the aisle from our family," Pat said. "We're sitting on the right side of the podium, and you can sit on the other side."

I was momentarily baffled. *We're not all going to sit together?* I didn't know what to say to Pat, so I didn't respond at all.

After nearly everyone was seated—there were around five hundred people who came—I walked with my family toward the front of the sanctuary. We took our places in the second row on the left side, feeling the eyes of people in the pews watching us.

Just before the service started, my three children and the Feasel side of the family walked in and sat across the aisle from us. This was perhaps the lowest moment of my life. I couldn't believe I wasn't sitting close to my children. I began sobbing.

I tried not to weep out loud. Mom, sitting next to me, took my hand. I sobbed even louder. *I should be next to Sean. I should be holding Sarah's hand. I should have an arm around Spencer.* It was sad and upsetting to be shunned at the funeral of the man I had been married to for many years.

The service featured tributes from my three children, his brother, Greg, and several of Grant's college roommates and close friends.

Sean, as the oldest, told several touching stories about asking his father to come to his first-grade class for career day and how his classmates were certainly impressed to have a larger-than-life NFL player in their midst. He said that if he could send a telegram—or maybe an e-mail, he joked—to his father, he would say this:

"Dad, it was such an honor and a blessing to be your son. You taught me so much. I will do everything in my power to continue your legacy. You will be greatly missed down here, but you will always be my daddy and my hero."

Sarah said, "Saying thank you doesn't seem like enough, but thank you for teaching me where to find the source of lasting strength. The way you loved Jesus was inspiring to everyone who knew you."

Spencer was more poignant. "Grant Earl Feasel was my hero. I know I lost my dad when he was only fifty-two years of age and I was only eighteen, but I know this has happened to make me the man and father I will someday be."

Those were touching tributes from three adult children who loved their father. There was no doubt in my mind that Grant loved our children. He was always soft-spoken with them and never raised his voice. For that, I was grateful.

I was not given the opportunity to speak that day. But if I had been asked, I would have said something like this:

> I'm so proud of our children and how they stood up today and shared the kind words they said about their dad. If you didn't know Grant well, he was a smart, kind, and soft individual. He was the most handsome guy I thought I had ever seen. He was a man of his word, and he was an organized man. That's how I remember him being when we married.
>
> Even though there were times that got really tense and we didn't stay married, I want everyone to hold on to the memory they have of Grant. If you were one of Grant's coaches at ACU, remember Grant that way. If you played football with Grant, then remember how upstanding he was and how dedicated he was on and off the field.
>
> For me, I want to remember the good things about Grant. Yes, we had some difficult years, and it was hard to live with somebody who had an addiction that took a huge toll on our family and our marriage. That doesn't mean I didn't love Grant. I loved him. He was my spouse whom I cared about deeply until the very end.
>
> But I don't want my reflection to have anything to do with the way you remember Grant. If you have an awesome memory of him, keep that memory of him because he was a great guy.

When the service was over, the Feasel family and my three children walked out first. I didn't want to talk to anyone until I hugged my children. Their party retreated to a waiting room off the foyer, where they could compose themselves before meeting the public.

I caught Sarah and Spencer as they were leaving the family room, and we exchanged hugs. Then I saw Sean inside, and he embraced me as much as I embraced him. I once again expressed how sorry I was that Grant had died.

I returned to the foyer, where well-wishers immediately surrounded me. They formed a line, and they wanted two things from me: a hug and an answer to the question, "What happened to Grant?"

Many of these wonderful friends were from the world of football or our days at Abilene Christian. They remembered Grant as a gladiator on the gridiron, someone whose size and strength were Samson-like, and yet he had died at the relatively young age of fifty-two, which was twenty-six years less than the average life expectancy of a US male. They were hoping for answers.

Among those who lined up to have a word with me were his professors in college, his football coaches, and teammates in the NFL. Many, of course, did not know that we were divorced and wondered why I wasn't sitting with my children. When they asked what happened to Grant, I didn't mince words: "Grant was an alcoholic." I said it exactly like that, no beating around the bush. Then I added, "Our marriage and family suffered greatly because of his drinking. I did the best I could."

Wade Wilson, the quarterbacks coach with the Dallas Cowboys, played against Grant in college while at East Texas State and was a teammate of Grant's when we were in Minnesota. He looked me in the face and said, "I'm just blown away. I never saw Grant drink more than a beer. Grant loved you. Grant loved his kids more than anything in the world. I can't even picture how Grant's life ended like this."

I know, I know.

Jeff Kemp, the Seahawks quarterback and holder who Grant snapped the ball to for field goals and extra points, also patiently waited in line with his wife, Stacy, to ask me what happened.

"I can't wrap my mind around what happened to Grant," he said after I told him that his old teammate had become an alcoholic drug addict. "Grant was such an awesome guy."

I know, I know.

I'll never forget Jeff's last words to me. "Cyndy," he said, "I don't know or understand what's happened here, but the only way to heal is to be completely transparent," he said.

And that's what I'm choosing to do.

A SEARCH FOR ANSWERS

A month or so after Grant's death, Greg Feasel called my father. Greg was the executor of Grant's estate, and he had donated Grant's brain to science to test for the presence of chronic traumatic encephalopathy (CTE), the progressive degenerative disease of the brain found mainly in athletes with a history of repetitive brain trauma, including concussions and concussive hits to the head.

CTE was in the news because a number of retired NFL players were committing suicide and leaving grim notes behind like the one Chicago Bears safety Dave Duerson wrote on February 17, 2011. He had shot himself in the heart and left a message to his ex-wife Alicia that said, "Please see that my brain is given to the NFL's brain bank."

So even though I'd heard of CTE, I didn't know much. Then I remembered that Keli McGregor, one of Grant's closest friends from the NFL and Greg's boss at the Colorado Rockies, who died suddenly in 2010, had his brain tested for CTE. The results came back positive. I'm sure Greg was thinking that if Keli had CTE, then it was entirely possible that Grant could have had the same degenerative disease.

Before Grant's body was cremated, a pathologist removed his brain, eyes, and spinal cord, which were shipped to the Concussion Legacy Foundation (formerly known as the Sports Legacy Institute) in Boston. The mission of the institute is to advance the study, treatment, and prevention of the effects of brain trauma in athletes and other at-risk groups.

The Concussion Legacy Foundation was working in concert with the National Institutes of Health (NIH) and the Boston University

CTE Center to study chronic traumatic encephalopathy, which can begin months, years, or decades after the last brain trauma—such as a concussion—or the end of active athletic involvement. CTE can only be tested for postmortem, when scientists study the brain's tissues for a buildup of an abnormal protein known as tau, which was becoming associated with memory loss, confusion, impaired judgment, impulse control problems, aggression, depression, and progressive dementia.

Greg wanted our family to know that Grant's brain, spinal cord, and eyes were being put under a microscope, so to speak.

The test results would change my life

CHAPTER 19

GAME CHANGER

On a spring day in 2013, Sean and Greg flew to Boston to meet with Dr. Ann McKee, a professor of pathology at the Boston University School of Medicine and chief neuropathologist for the VA-BU-CLF Brain Bank.

The VA-BU-CLF Brain Bank—the abbreviations standing for Veterans Administration, Boston University, and Concussion Legacy Foundation—opened in 2008 and became the first repository in the world dedicated to the study of CTE. The Brain Bank was the first research organization to discover CTE in athletes ranging from football to soccer, ice hockey, and lacrosse.

Sean and Greg traveled to Boston because testing on Grant's brain, spinal cord, and eyes was complete, and the results were in. In a sense, they were hearing from arguably the foremost expert in the world on CTE. Dr. McKee was on the forefront of neurodegenerative diseases, with a primary focus on the role of tau protein in the brain cells.

I would've loved to join them in Boston to hear the test results myself, but that wasn't in the playbook. I was grateful that Sean called my dad to share a summary of their meeting. Sean said that Dr. McKee began by explaining that CTE is a degenerative brain disease found in many athletes with a history of repetitive brain injuries. There is some randomness, however, because not all football players come down with CTE, just as some people can chain-smoke cigarettes all their lives and never get cancer. On the flip side, just as nominal smokers can quit but still develop lung cancer, an athlete—no matter what sport he or she plays—is at risk for CTE from a few concussions or jarring hits to the head.

Dr. McKee explained that the neurodegenerative condition of CTE is not instigated by old age or genetics but by injury to the brain. The majority of CTE cases express themselves via behavioral and emotional changes such as depression, antisocial behavior, lack of impulse control, and fiscal and legal irresponsibility.

Concussions and "dings" on the football field that aren't allowed to heal thoroughly activate the tau protein, which then moves throughout healthy brain cells. When the frontal lobe—the seat of socialization, emotional intelligence, and rational thinking—becomes affected, the brain deteriorates over time. Memory loss and confusion become more prevalent.

Following that preamble, Dr. McKee next turned her attention to Grant's test results. After explaining that CTE diagnostic severity had a ranking system of 1 to 4, with 4 being the highest, she declared that Grant's brain was a Stage 3.

I wasn't sure what to think when my father relayed this information to me. Was Stage 3 bad or really bad? Greg and Sean had the same question and wondered how Grant's number compared to other football players who had CTE. Dr. McKee commented that Grant's results were "worse than John Doe's" and "equal to Bobby Doe's."

Dr. McKee used aliases out of respect for the families. Since the highest-profile examples of CTE, up to that time, were Junior Seau and Dave Duerson, one can infer that one of them was "John Doe" and the other was "Bobby Doe."

Then Dr. McKee delivered the most stunning news of all: Grant's brain stem was the most damaged she had ever seen. Furthermore, the most severely damaged parts of his brain were the areas affecting impulse, self-control, and organization.

I thought about the Grant who made sure his medical school test preparation books were stacked perfectly next to a mug containing pens and pencils, the Grant who always put his car keys in the same place and was the most organized man I knew. He had become the Grant who left unopened mail and important papers strewn around his office and could never keep up with his expense reports. The days of a tidy desk disappeared along with Grant's ability to keep track of a checkbook or his credit card spending.

Regarding impulse and self-control, Grant certainly gave free rein to the impulse to drink and gulp painkillers while failing to exercise any self-control regarding the amounts he was taking. His careful, methodical way of going through life was left behind when CTE gained a foothold.

Dr. McKee said Grant's brain showed no structural damage due to his alcoholism, but his alcohol abuse over many years produced liver and kidney failure, which was his cause of death. She added that CTE and alcoholism were parallel issues and one may not necessarily affect the other. Since Grant was above average in intelligence, she conjectured that when he was no longer on "top of his game" from the concussions and body slams, then behavioral and emotional changes led to severe depression—a by-product of CTE. Abusing alcohol was his coping mechanism.

Regarding the last point, my dad told me a story about the time when he visited Grant during his short stay in rehab in 2010. "I asked Grant to share with me why he began drinking," my dad said. "He explained that football injuries to his knees and back were painful. He said he tried various painkillers, but they gave him nausea. He learned that drinking vodka dulled the pain best. He did not specifically tell me how long he had been drinking before becoming addicted."

Which raises the question: Which came first, CTE or his addictions to alcohol and painkillers?

I believe that CTE came first. Grant had often described to me how much his head hurt after getting knocked around for four quarters. He once memorably described to a *Seattle Times* reporter that a "stinger" he received in one game made him feel "like somebody had opened my skin up and poured hot lava down my neck."

Throughout his playing career, Grant was handed a small plastic bag with several Vicodin pills after NFL games because he needed the painkillers to dull the sharp pains in his head, neck, and knees. This practice led to a lifelong dependence on painkillers. Once Grant retired, the pain meds weren't easy to get, which presented a problem. Coors Light and Jack Daniel's, however, were readily available any time he dropped by a liquor store. After Grant opened the door to Demon Booze, the tentacles of addiction gripped him tight and wouldn't let go.

The revelation that Grant had CTE was a game changer for me. I now had a much better understanding of the underlying reasons for his outrageous behavior. That didn't—and couldn't—excuse him for the way he belittled and abused me all those years, but this news gave me an explanation and context.

Greg mailed my dad a DVD that he received from Dr. McKee, and it explained to laypeople what CTE was all about. I watched the documentary with rapt attention as the narrator related CTE to the game of football and provided a time line of specific examples of what CTE does.

After viewing the documentary, I did my own research on CTE, scouring the Internet for articles and research. I found tons of information at the Concussion Legacy Foundation website. I read *Head Games: Football's Concussion Crisis* by Chris Nowinski, one of the first books to sound the alarm about the growing concussion crisis in sports.

I had flashbacks whenever I delved deeply into the topic of CTE. I became emotional and experienced clammy, sweaty skin. I wept and mourned the years Grant and I lost and the deep pain we went through.

I thought about what Grant endured and how his head hurt, his neck throbbed, his knees bothered him, and how alcohol slowly destroyed his liver and kidneys. I thought about how our children lost their father way too young and the emotional holes in their hearts.

We all lost someone we loved when Grant died. I lost my husband. The kids lost their dad. And the Feasels lost a son and a brother. It was all because of CTE.

With everything that happened, I have to ask myself: *Could I have stayed with Grant, knowing what I know now?*

The answer is no because Grant had become unmanageable. He wouldn't or couldn't commit to getting better at a rehab facility or completing an AA program. By the time I drove away, he was too far gone—a shell of himself. He was out of control, and there was no one who could help him. I left for my own sanity so I wouldn't end up driving off a cliff like Thelma and Louise.

Unfortunately, I couldn't have known beforehand that Grant had CTE because a diagnosis is only possible after death by postmortem neuropathological analysis. There is no known way to use MRIs, CAT scans, or other brain-imaging methods to diagnose CTE.

I'm heartbroken that Grant had CTE. I loved him. I loved him in spite of his addictions, and I loved him in spite of his CTE. I'm anguished and sad that our lives came to this and he fell into such a downward spiral after his NFL career ended.

WHO ELSE IS LIKE ME?

I don't believe my story is unique. There are roughly twelve thousand living former NFL players, and around four thousand of them are suing the NFL over head injuries, according to a *Washington Times* database. In other words, one out of every three retired players is seeking a settlement for concussion-related brain injuries, which tells me there are thousands of women who could tell stories similar to mine.

Junior Seau was one of the greatest linebackers in NFL history. His intensity on the field and on the practice field, as well as his knack for making big plays, made him one of the game's biggest stars. There's a revealing story in the book *Junior Seau: The Life and Death of a Football Icon* by Jim Trotter in which Junior—during *training camp*—popped fullback Fred McCrary so violently that their helmet-to-helmet hit left a three-inch crack across the bridge of McCrary's helmet. The fullback saw white spots after the initial collision. Throughout the rest of the day, McCrary's head throbbed as he struggled with his equilibrium.

When McCrary ran into Junior that night in the dorms, they compared notes. "My head is on fire, but we can't tell James," Junior said, referring to team trainer James Collins.

Why am I not surprised?

Dave Duerson was a brilliant student athlete at Notre Dame and an eleven-year safety for the Chicago Bears, New York Giants, and Phoenix Cardinals, as well as the 1987 NFL Man of the Year. Where Grant's post-NFL life can be categorized as inertia, Duerson was going places: he bought a meat-packing company, which he rebranded Duerson Foods, and sold sausage to mega-clients like Burger King and McDonald's. Throughout his post-NFL days, he remained involved on the NFL Players Association's retirement board.

But Duerson wasn't as adept in the business world as he thought he was, and his company hemorrhaged money. There were screaming rages with family members who were part of the business, and Duerson was arrested for pushing his wife against a hotel wall near the Notre Dame campus.

On a February day in 2011, while alone in his luxury Sunny Isles Beach condo in Miami, fifty-year-old Duerson sent texts to family members and finished several handwritten notes that said, "Please see that my brain is given to the NFL's brain bank."

Then he removed all of his clothes, climbed under the sheets of his bed, and held a .38 Special handgun to his chest. A squeeze of the trigger, and his life was over.

Junior Seau committed suicide in much the same way—shooting himself at his home on the beach in Oceanside, California, just a few miles north of DeWayne and Pat's house in Carlsbad where we spent so many vacations. Seau, alone in his home, went into his daughter's bedroom, placed the tip of a handgun against his heart, and pulled the trigger. He was found slumped on a queen-size bed. Like Duerson, Seau wanted to be sure his brain was intact to determine whether he had CTE.

They are not the only NFL players to have committed suicide. The following players killed themselves and were found to have CTE:

- Jovan Belcher shot and killed his girlfriend and mother of their child in December 2012, then drove to the Kansas City Chiefs' practice facility, where he shot and killed himself in the parking lot.
- Adrian Robinson, who played for several seasons in the NFL, hung himself. He was twenty-five.
- Andre Waters, who played a decade in the NFL at safety, shot himself in the head in 2006. He was forty-four years old.
- In 2009, Shane Dronett, a defensive lineman, pulled a gun on his wife but killed himself instead.
- Terry Long, an offensive lineman for the Steelers at the same time Grant played, drank antifreeze to kill himself in 2005. He was forty-five years old.
- Ray Easterling, a safety with the Atlanta Falcons during the 1970s, shot himself in 2012 at the age of sixty-two.
- Paul Oliver, another safety who played for the San Diego Chargers as recently as 2011, shot and killed himself in 2013. He was only twenty-nine years old.

I could describe other suicides, and there will be more. Suicides are just the tip of the iceberg since a vast majority of former players do not take their lives with their own hand but instead prematurely die for other reasons—such as heart failure, cancer, Alzheimer's disease, dementia, or end-stage liver disease. What's disconcerting but unsurprising to me is that the more the NFL Brain Bank examines the brains of deceased football players, the more of a slam dunk CTE becomes.

In 2015, researchers with the Department of Veteran Affairs and Boston University found CTE in eighty-seven of ninety-one former NFL players tested. That's 96 percent. But here's a statistic that should make every parent sit up and take notice: According to the same report, researchers found CTE in 131 of 165 football players who played for pro, semipro, college, and high school teams. That's 79 percent.

Dr. McKee, who issued the report, said, "People think that we're blowing this out of proportion, that this [CTE] is a very rare disease and that we're sensationalizing it. My response is that from where I sit, this is a very real disease. We have no problem identifying it in hundreds of players."

The NFL has a real problem on its hands, although The League has in the past adopted a "see no evil, hear no evil" attitude when it comes to concussions. Steve Kroft of *60 Minutes*, in a lead-in to a 2015 segment on concussions in football, said, "Not since football was nearly banned a hundred years ago has the sport been under the microscope the way it is today, and all of it has to do with matters of the brain." The *60 Minutes* report outlined how the NFL—a multibillion dollar industry—is changing its rules, trying to reinvent equipment, and even funding scientific research that could endanger its future as the country's most popular sport.

Further evidence that the NFL is coming around happened in March 2016, when the NFL's senior vice president of health and safety policy, Jeff Miller, acknowledged for the first time the connection between football-related brain trauma and CTE. Speaking before the House Committee on Energy and Commerce, Miller was asked if there is a link between football and the CTE research coming from Dr. McKee and her colleagues.

"Well, certainly Dr. McKee's research shows that a number of retired NFL players were diagnosed with CTE, so the answer to that question is certainly yes," Miller told lawmakers. "But there's also a number of questions that come with that."

The best step the NFL has taken is instituting a "concussion protocol" and having spotters in the press box who are looking for one of seven observable signs of a concussion:

- any loss of consciousness
- slow to get up following a hit to the head
- motor coordination and balance problems (stumbles, trips, or labored movement)
- a blank or vacant look
- disorientation (unsure of where he is on the field)
- clutching of head after contact
- visible facial injury

The NFL spotter program was implemented in 2012 after quarterback Colt McCoy was viciously decked by Pittsburgh Steelers linebacker James Harrison and laid out on the field for a *long* time. Colt was half dragged off the field, nauseated and not knowing who he was. Team trainers gave him a perfunctory once-over, pronounced him good to go, and Colt trotted back into the huddle after missing two plays.

With the game on the line—it was late in the fourth quarter—Colt under-threw the ball into the end zone and was picked off. Game over. It's a game that Colt doesn't remember playing.

His father, Brad McCoy—who happened to play football with Grant at Abilene Christian—criticized the Browns for not neuro-testing Colt after the crushing blow, which was later determined to be a severe concussion. "After the game, the Browns made sure Colt's interview was brief and he couldn't face the lights in his press conference," Brad said. "The TV lights and the stadium lights were killing him. Why would you say he was fine? That makes it even worse."

The jury is still out on whether the NFL's spotter program is working the way it should, but at least it's a strong step in the right direction.

SOME PARENTAL ADVICE

So, knowing what I know about CTE—since I've read a great deal after learning Grant was Stage 3—how do I feel about boys playing football? Or boys and girls playing other sports where concussions are possible?

I'll start by saying that Grant was adamant about our two boys not playing Pop Warner football when they were eight, nine, and ten years old. He didn't allow Sean and Spencer to play organized football until they were in fifth grade because he thought their bodies were too underdeveloped.

But that doesn't fully address the issue of whether you should allow your son to play football. If I were doing it all over again, I would first research and read up on everything I could about concussions and youth sports. I would talk to other parents, the team trainers on high school football games, and former players.

You must educate yourself on what's happening to your children regardless of the sport or the level they compete in, whether it's high school sports, travel teams, club sports, or neighborhood leagues. For example, you could go online and do a search for "CTE and football" or "concussions in soccer" and learn what the research says.

Did you know that more than a dozen high school football players die each year from head, neck, and spine injuries? Or that concussions in children are more serious because developing brains need extra time and rest to heal?

Ask these questions and others. I want to spare your son or daughter from unnecessary concussions that could have severe impacts on their health and impulse control in their adult years.

CHAPTER 20

EXTRA POINT

I've often thought that Grant's final words to me—wishing he'd never played football—should be inscribed on his grave marker in Barstow, where Grant's ashes are buried next to three generations of Feasels. Because at the end of the day—and the end of this story—football proved to be an irresistible siren call.

Think of what happened to Grant growing up. When he was in youth football, he heard adults say, *You've got some real talent there, son. Just wait until you play high school football.*

And then Grant took the field for the Barstow Aztecs and became a big deal in a small California desert city. He heard the adults in his life say, *Look how good you are. You're one of the best linemen in Barstow High history. You're an All-League stud. You can play college football.*

College scouting wasn't as sophisticated in 1978 as it is today with "five-star" recruits and digitized video highlights that can be easily attached to an e-mail. Because of Grant's lack of exposure growing up in the remote Mojave Desert, he could only get smaller schools to look at him. He said yes to Abilene Christian because his brother, Greg, paved the way and Grant was offered a scholarship.

So Grant played center at Abilene Christian, and once again, coaches and alumni boosters told him, *You're one of the greatest linemen in ACU history. You're first All-American in Division II. You've got the size that NFL coaches drool over. You can play on Sundays.*

And Grant dreamed of playing in jammed stadiums with seventy thousand screaming fans and a national TV audience looking on that totaled in the tens of millions, of having cameras and microphones thrust in front of him, of being part of an NFL locker room and experiencing the incredible bond between those who'd reached the summit of the most popular sport in America. All of that swirled in Grant's mind.

When professional football beckoned, Grant gave up his goal of becoming a dentist or a doctor. He accepted that Faustian bargain, unaware that football demanded a heavy price: crippled knees that limited his ability to walk, horrible headaches and terrible neck pains, an inability to think cognitively or in a productive manner, his unavailability as a dad to his children, his damaged relationship with me, and ultimately many years of his life.

And what did Grant get in return?

Sure, he heard the roar of the crowd and received athletic glory. He was paid handsomely, though that money disappeared. He was part of the ESPN SportsCenter highlights show every Sunday night. He saw his name in the sports pages and watched clips of himself being interviewed by local TV reporters. He was a charter member of the Ultimate Guy Club, and no one could take that away from him.

But fame was fleeting. I can guarantee you that one hour after Grant took off his Seahawks uniform for the last time, he was forgotten by the Seahawk coaching staff, the fans, the media, and the NFL.

At thirty-two, Grant should have had his whole life in front of him. Instead, his physical body was permanently injured—a pair of bad knees, a neck that killed him, a back that protested, and a brain clogged with tau protein.

Do I blame football for what happened to Grant? Yes, because there can be no other conclusion. Football—especially the savage game played at the line of scrimmage—is a violent, head-banging game that caused the concussions that produced the CTE that led to the addictions. But Grant loved playing the game and didn't want to stop until his body gave out.

Life did not end well for Grant. Our marriage ended horribly. Our children were severely impacted by what they saw growing up. I watched the man of my dreams slip further away every day in front of my eyes.

By the world's standards, I face a bleak future, having lost everything financially. Deep emotional scars will likely keep me in therapy for the rest of my life. I live modestly in a duplex and subsist on a schoolteacher's salary.

But I refuse to give up. I'm excited about tomorrow. I have parents and close family who love me unconditionally. I have a roof over my head and can pay my bills, but better than that, I have the greatest possession anyone can have: the hope for eternal life with Jesus Christ. I'm relying on what God tells me in Jeremiah 29:11:

> "I'll show up and take care of you as I promised and bring you back home. I know what I'm doing. I have it all planned out—plans to take care of you, not abandon you, plans to give you the future you hope for."

In the years I have left, I know what my mission in life is: to tell other parents about the dangers of CTE and playing head-banging sports. Grant missed his real gifts and destiny in this world, but I'm still here. I believe he'd be cheering me on to share his story as a cautionary tale of what can happen when you play a sport you love but that has inherent risks that wreak tremendous physical damage.

So Grant, I know where you are—in heaven with our everlasting Father. You're whole now and living in peace.

That's the Grant I can't wait to see again.

AFTERWORD

by Daniel G. Amen, M.D.

New York Times Bestselling Author of
Change Your Brain, Change Your Life

I applaud Cyndy Feasel for the strength she showed in sharing her harrowing story about a topic that is not only in the news today but is also a growing focus within the Amen Clinics, a group of medical centers that I founded.

We specialize in the treatment of mood and behavior disorders and employ brain SPECT (single photon emission computed tomography) imaging to diagnose and treat our patients. I wish we could have helped Grant Feasel because I would imagine that his condition was similar to many of the ex-NFL athletes we have cared for in the past.

One of those was USC football star Anthony Davis, who came to see me as a patient about a decade ago. In his midfifties at the time, AD—as the sports world called him—was worried that a diminished mental state was in his future. He'd witnessed cognitive problems in other retired football players.

Anthony had played six seasons of professional football and had taken his share of hits, even as a swivel-hipped running back. He is best known for scoring six touchdowns for the Trojans against rival Notre Dame back in 1972, prompting Fighting Irish fans to plaster his picture on the walkways of the Notre Dame campus so that they could step all over him.

Following testing in our clinic, we determined that AD's brain showed clear evidence of trauma to his prefrontal cortex and left temporal lobe. We immediately put him on a stringent diet of brain-healthy foods (low-glycemic fruits and vegetables, high-fiber carbohydrates, high-quality proteins, and healthy fats) and nutritional supplements targeting inflammation, blood flow, blood sugar stabilization, and antioxidant support. Within five months, AD reported improvements in memory, energy, focus, and judgment. His brain got better.

Immensely pleased with his results, Anthony asked me to speak to the Los Angeles chapter of the Retired NFL Players Association and talk about good habits for brain health.

When I addressed the group in January 2009, the levels of depression and dementia in the retired players I met horrified me. One player asked me the same question *six times*! These former football greats desperately needed answers to questions about the link between playing football and experiencing brain damage. My research team at Amen Clinics, together with scientists from University of California, Irvine and Thomas Jefferson University, tackled this timely issue. In 2011, my colleagues and I published the first and largest brain-imaging study of one hundred active and retired NFL players from twenty-seven teams and all positions. Over 90 percent showed clear evidence of traumatic brain injury (TBI).

Since then, we've put together a database of nearly two hundred players that includes retired Minnesota Viking offensive guard Brent Boyd, who complained of headaches, depression, fatigue, dizziness, cognitive dysfunction, alcohol issues, and relationship problems when he came to see me.

Brent had suffered multiple concussions in his football career. His Vikings teammate Joe Senser told me he heard one of the hits on Brent all the way across the field. Brent spent many years dealing with post-concussive syndrome. "It was hell," he said, "to experience decades of being called 'lazy and crazy' by friends and loved ones, not to mention employers—and then internalizing it and believing it myself." Prior to the concussions, Brent had always been a highly motivated self-starter, graduating with honors at UCLA while playing football.

His SPECT scans showed clear evidence of brain damage. He later wrote to me, "I am eternally grateful to you for finally correctly diagnosing my problem and putting an end to the self-talk and put-downs by others. I had been so embarrassed by my condition that for over a decade I had cut myself off from friends, family, and ex-teammates and crawled under my blanket to die." In 2007, Brent was the first NFL player to testify before Congress about brain injuries in football, especially regarding the ramifications for younger players.

Many people do not know that the brain is soft, has the consistency of soft butter, and is housed in a hard skull that has many sharp bony ridges. The brain is not anchored to the skull, however, so it floats in cerebrospinal fluid. This means that helmets, which can do a good job of protecting you against skull fractures, cannot protect you from brain damage.

Hard hits propel delicate brain tissue to slam against hard, knifelike edges within the skull, causing bleeding, bruising, tearing, and scarring, especially to the prefrontal cortex and temporal lobes. These hits can cause trouble, even without a loss of consciousness or any outward symptoms of concussion. Brain damage may be occurring insidiously without the brain ever telling you that it's in trouble, which can ruin your life.

Since preventing brain trauma is key to living a healthy life, I do not recommend that your children play football. The game's too dangerous for delicate brains. You really want to protect their brains because when the brain works right, they have a much better chance of doing well in life, but when the brain is troubled, they're much more likely to have issues, especially later in life.

In the last couple of years, I've seen evidence that more and more parents are keeping their kids out of football. I live in Southern California, where some of the powerhouse high school football programs are seeing big drops in participation. Los Angeles Loyola High, an all-boys school with 1,300 students, recently had the fewest number of freshman players in two decades. Significant drops were also seen at Notre Dame High, Bishop Alemany High, and Crespi Carmelite High, where I played football forty-seven years ago. Nationwide, participation in high school football has declined in five of the last six years, according to the National Federation of State High School Associations.

As hard as one may try to justify the benefits of football—the lessons of hard work, the value of teamwork, and dealing with adversity—it's impossible to ignore reality: brain injuries are as much a part of football as the coin flip before the start of the game.

If you have children or teens who want to play football, first tell them why it is a terrible idea and then tell them, "Absolutely not. Your brain is involved in everything you do and everything you are. When it works right, you work right; when it is troubled—for whatever reason—you are much more likely to have trouble in your life."

Your child's brain health will either allow them to live as happy, healthy, effective adults or as ones more prone to depression, dementia, relationship problems, or legal trouble—just as poignantly described by Cyndy Feasel in *After the Cheering Stops*.

ACKNOWLEDGMENTS

In 2015, I read *Still LoLo*, a book by fashion journalist Lauren "LoLo" Scruggs, who exited a small plane piloted by a family friend and inadvertently walked into the still-moving propeller.

She survived several major surgeries but lost her left hand and her left eye, but she did not lose her determination to overcome the new challenges set in her path. I found *Still LoLo* to be an encouraging read at a time when I needed inspiration.

I noticed that Lauren collaborated with writer Marcus Brotherton, who did a beautiful job of sharing her story in a compelling and fiercely beautiful way. Ever since my former husband, Grant, died in 2012, my therapists, Bill and Ranee Gumm—who knew my story better than anyone else—had been encouraging me to share my experiences in a book. After reading *Still LoLo*, I thought Marcus Brotherton could help me.

I didn't know how to reach him, but I did find Marcus on Facebook, so I typed out a message to him. He immediately answered with a positive response in which he encouraged me to share the story you've just read. Marcus added that he had several other book projects going and couldn't help me, but he offered to pass along my message to his literary agent, Greg Johnson, of WordServe Literary Group in Highlands Ranch, Colorado.

Greg and I had a friendly conversation on the phone, and he mentioned that he happened to be traveling to Dallas on other business and wanted to meet me for breakfast to hear more about my story. For one hour at an airport hotel restaurant, Greg listened intently while I poured out my heart and described my desire to write a book about how CTE impacts football families. Greg then paired me with veteran author Mike Yorkey, who's done many sports-related books, and the results speak for themselves. I thank Mike for his tenderness in helping me walk through some very dark times while keeping in mind the redemptive nature of my story and my goal to help others.

That's why I'm grateful to Brian Hampton and his team at Thomas Nelson Publishers for saying yes to *After the Cheering Stops* and giving me a chance to get into the game. I'm appreciative to early readers like Ross Mitchell, Rebecca Trautvetter, Leah Firth, Shannon Bailey, and Nicole Yorkey for their comments as well as the proofing skills of Heidi Moss. Corky Trewin, a Seattle photographer and longtime veteran of NFL sidelines, provided the action photos of Grant. Adrianne Verheyen was a superb transcriber.

I must also acknowledge my parents, David and Martha Davy, who have modeled a lifetime of love and faith. My sisters Lori and Alisa and their families have been relentless in their love and support. Bill and Ranee Gumm, my Christian therapists, have held my hand while they talked me through the darkness to see the light.

To my many friends, including Melissa Barrow, Danny and Karen Miller, Russ and Susan Garrison and their son Kent, you know who you are and know exactly where you fit into my story. You played a significant role and blessed me in my darkest hours. I thank Lori Walker, who gave me her duplex for a year and paid for everything, including utilities, after I left Grant and moved out with some clothes and a few family photos. There were also anonymous persons who blessed me with faith-affirming gifts, like the time I arrived at my classroom and found an envelope on my desk. Inside were five one-hundred-dollar bills.

Thank you, God, for watching out for me and giving me peace that passes all understanding. Please guide me as I share *After the Cheering Stops* with others.

SOURCE MATERIAL

A Note to the Reader

"In addition, a study published in the *American Journal of Sports Medicine* showed that girls playing soccer . . ." from "Trends in Concussions Incidence in High School Sports: A Prospective 11-Year Study," a study by Andrew E. Lincoln, ScD., et al., published by the *American Journal of Sports Medicine*, 2011, and available at http://ajs.sagepub.com/content/early/2011/01/29/0363546510392326.

Chapter 9

"Joe Tofflemire died of heart failure at the age of forty-six . . ." from "Give Tofflemire Thought on Sunday," by John Blanchette, *The Spokesman-Review*, October 1, 2011, available at http://www.spokesman.com/stories/2011/oct/01/blanchette-give-tofflemire-thought-sunday/.

Chapter 14

"What I didn't know at the time was that Grant was entering the fourth and final progression of CTE symptoms . . ." from "Blanchette: Chronic Traumatic Encephalopathy Symptoms" by the Mayo Clinic Staff, available on the Mayo Clinic website at http://www.mayoclinic.org/diseases-conditions/chronic-traumatic-encephalopathy/basics/symptoms/con-20113581.

Chapter 19

"There are roughly twelve thousand living former NFL players . . ." from "Concussion Lawsuits Against NFL Shouldn't Be for Everyone," by Akbar

Gbajabiamila, NFL.com website, February 11, 2013, and available at http://www.nfl.com/news/story/0ap1000000137991/article/concussion-lawsuits-against-nfl-shouldnt-be-for-everyone.

"My head is on fire . . ." from the book *Junior Seau: The Life and Death of a Football Icon* by Jim Trotter (Houghton Mifflin Harcourt, 2015), page 109.

"In 2015, researchers with the Department of Veteran Affairs and Boston University found CTE . . ." from "Study Finds 96 Percent of Former NFL Players Had CTE," by Michael O'Keeffe, *New York Daily News*, September 18, 2015, available at http://www.nydailynews.com/sports/football/study-finds-96-percent-nfl-players-cte-article-1.2365865.

"People think that we're blowing this out of proportion . . ." from "Study Finds 96 Percent of Former NFL Players Had CTE," by Michael O'Keeffe, *New York Daily News*, September 18, 2015, and available at http://www.nydailynews.com/sports/football/study-finds-96-percent-nfl-players-cte-article-1.2365865.

"Steve Kroft of *60 Minutes*, in a lead-in to a 2015 segment on concussions . . ." from "Football and the Brain," the transcript for a November 15, 2015 segment on CBS's show *60 Minutes*, and available at http://www.cbsnews.com/news/football-and-the-brain-nfl-60-minutes/.

"Well, certainly Dr. McKee's research shows that a number of retired NFL players . . ." from "NFL Executive Acknowledges a Link Between Football-Related Head Trauma and CTE," by Sam Farmer and Nathan Fenno, *Los Angeles Times*, March 14, 2016, and available at http://www.latimes.com/sports/sportsnow/la-sp-nfl-cte-jeff-miller-20160314-story.html.

"After the game, the Browns made sure Colt's interview was brief . . ." from "Colt McCoy's Father Says McCoy Doesn't Remember Anything After Hit," by Mary Kay Cabot, *Cleveland.com*, December 9, 2011, and available at http://www.cleveland.com/browns/index.ssf/2011/12/colt_mccoys_father_says_mccoy.html.

ABOUT THE AUTHORS

C yndy Feasel, the author of *After the Cheering Stops*, is an art teacher at Fort Worth Christian School in North Richland Hills, Texas. She grew up in the Dallas suburb of Garland as the oldest of three daughters to David and Martha Davy.

She attended Abilene Christian University in Abilene, Texas, where she met Grant Feasel, a center on the Abilene Wildcats football team. After graduating with a degree in elementary art education and earning a master's in early childhood education, she became a primary school teacher and married Grant, who was drafted by the Baltimore Colts in 1983. For the next ten years, Grant played in the NFL, although he lost two seasons to knee injuries. In total, he played 117 games and was a three-year starter for the Seattle Seahawks.

Following Grant's retirement, the family moved back to the Dallas area, where Cyndy raised three children: Sean, Sarah, and Spencer. She returned to the classroom in the late 1990s and still teaches art classes from kindergarten to eighth grade students at Fort Worth Christian.

Cyndy makes her home in North Richland Hills, Texas. Her website is www.cyndyfeasel.com.

M ike Yorkey is the author or coauthor of one hundred books with more than two million copies in print. He has collaborated with

Chicago Cubs second baseman Ben Zobrist and his wife, Julianna, a Christian music artist, in *Double Play*; Washington Redskins quarterback Colt McCoy and his father, Brad, in *Growing Up Colt*; San Francisco Giants pitcher Dave Dravecky in *Called Up*; San Diego Chargers placekicker Rolf Benirschke in *Alive & Kicking*; tennis star Michael Chang in *Holding Serve*; and paralyzed Rutgers' defensive tackle Eric LeGrand in *Believe: My Faith and the Tackle That Changed My Life*. Mike is also the coauthor of the internationally bestselling Every Man's Battle series with Steve Arterburn and Fred Stoeker.

He and his wife, Nicole, are the parents of two adult children and make their home in Encinitas, California.

Mike's website is www.mikeyorkey.com.

INVITE CYNDY FEASEL TO SPEAK AT YOUR CHURCH OR COMMUNITY EVENT

Cyndy Feasel is a dynamic and emotional speaker with a passion to share her experiences about living with an NFL player who developed CTE and the life lessons she learned. Cyndy is available to speak at men's and women's weekend conferences and vacation retreats.

If you, your church, or your community organization would like Cyndy to come speak at your event, contact:

Phil Van Horn
Integrity Sports Agency LLC
301 N. Lake Ave, 7th Floor
Pasadena, CA 91101
(818) 517-5880 cell
BallPhild@gmail.com

If you would like to purchase bulk copies of *After the Cheering Stops*, please call 1-800-251-4000 ext. 1480 or visit www.thomasnelson.com.